Shall W

Waiting for Mr. Right...
From One Single to Another

Amanda Wilders

ISBN 978-1-64114-685-2 (Paperback)
ISBN 978-1-64114-686-9 (Digital)

Christian Faith Publishing, Inc.
296 Chestnut Street
Meadville, PA 16335
www.christianfaithpublishing.com

Printed in the United States of America

Shall We Dance?

Waiting for Mr. Right...
From One Single to Another

CONTENTS

ACKNOWLEDGMENTS

There are a lot of amazing people who have helped me through my journey thus far. To name all of them would probably fill this entire book, so I'd like to thank my family and just a few of the women who have seen me through and mentored me along the way.

My family is one of the greatest gifts God has blessed me with. You are always there for me no matter what life throws. I'm so excited as we continue to grow. We're our own kind of crazy, but I love it!

Thank you Mommy! Michelle Wilders, you have been my best friend over the years. You are my biggest fan. You have always encouraged me to dream big and never settle for less than God's very best for me.

Melly, you are one of the coolest people I know, and I so value your opinion. You are beautiful, compassionate, kind, and loving. I am so proud of you. You're a good mommy—James and Elijah adore you. You are following your heart and have become an amazing woman. Thanks for always standing up for me and wanting the best for me. I am grateful for your love and friendship and couldn't ask for a better sister!

Aunt Karen, Mona Ponder, and Nancy Farnsworth are just some of the many mighty prayer warriors that always took up arms for me. Thank you for your prayers and encouragement to guard my heart, follow my dreams, and never give up!

I'd like to give a big thank you to Jackie Vaggalis, who has walked with me for years of waiting for the right man to come along. I remember once turning someone down for a Valentine's date and then calling you upset because I was worried he could have been "the one," and I messed things up. You were very patient with my young self. You prayed for me, encouraged me, and then kindly said, "Amanda, you're not an old maid!" I wonder if you'd say the same thing today about ten years later, ha! I am confident that he was not right for me, and I thank you for helping me through that and other dramas over the years. You have prayed for me, laughed with me, hugged me, and cried with me. You and your family opened up your home to me in the most difficult time of my life and helped me through. I will always treasure that.

I am so grateful for my time at Hillsong International Leadership College and want to say a huge thanks to all of the trainers, pastors, and friendships that have forever impacted my life. Thank you Pastor Brian and Bobbie Houston for obeying the call of God and starting Hillsong Church. I am so blessed to have sat under your teaching, as well as Pastors Joel and Julia A'bell.

A special thanks to Tina Brown for allowing me the privilege to serve with you and get to know you. You are diligent and such a hard worker who's made a difference in my life and so many others.

Katie Dodson, you gave me a much-needed perspective shift during my time at Hillsong. After a meeting with you, my entire vision for the future was expanded. I went from hoping for a specific position in life to dreaming bigger and not limiting myself or what God wants to do through me. Thank you for your contagious joy and for always being genuine about who you are. Thank you for sharing your time and wisdom with me and so many others.

Margaret Stunt, you challenged me to look beyond myself and be intentional about sharing the love of God with those around me. Thank you for pushing me outside my comfort zone.

I'd like to give a special shout-out to Destiny Worship Center and all of my small group gals—especially our "Talk-a-latte" group! There were so many good times, amazing moments with friends, and answered prayers. Love you all!

To the many who have impacted my life and were not mentioned here, you are not forgotten. You are treasured beyond words. You make a huge difference in people's lives and will continue to do so as you follow our amazing God. Thank you!

INTRODUCTION

There are many books out there written by Christian women who have been through the ringer when it comes to men. Some share stories of how hard it was being single, but it was worth the wait. Others tell how they dated all the wrong men, but when they finally surrendered it to God, they eventually found the perfect man for them. I recently read a book by Jackie Kendall called *A Man Worth Waiting For.* The book encourages you to hold out for a man worth waiting for and gives descriptions of what she calls a "Bozo" versus a "Boaz." As she shares of her trials and triumphs and how she found her "Boaz," she urges single women today to wait for the right man to come along. I highly recommend the book and very much enjoyed it, but I admittedly had this thought as I read, "Easy for her to say. She's found her man!" (Hey, I'm only human.☺)

After this thought and a heart check, I felt that there may be other women who would like to hear from someone who is in the same season of life they are in—someone who currently deals with the issues, emotions, temptations, and struggles they deal with. Hence, this book, "Shall We Dance," took form.

I pray that as you read, the Lord will encourage your heart to be steadfast in seeking God and never settle for less than God's best, especially when it comes to the husband He has in mind for you.

Never settle for less than God's best for you...

CHAPTER 1

ONCE UPON A TIME

*"Once upon a time there lived a
handsome prince…"*

—Anonymous

So many of our favorite stories when we are young girls begin with "once upon a time…" We know right away that it will be a magical story filled with adventure, romance and, most importantly, ending in "and they all lived happily ever after." I believe all of us desire our own happily ever after and have daydreamed about what that would look like.

I started writing this book as a single young woman with a word from the Lord and a hope in my heart. Like many single ladies, I have the dream of one day being "swept off my feet by Prince Charming." Now, I fully understand that there is no such thing as the perfect man, but I do believe with all my heart that God has a man in mind who will be a perfect fit for each of us.

There is someone out there that God knows will encourage us in our pursuit of Him; someone who will passionately serve God alongside us and will walk side by side with us in the calling He's placed on our lives. So let me start by telling you a bit of my story. Several years ago, I had a boyfriend, my first boyfriend to be exact. He was a great guy. I met him at church, and he loved God with all his heart, not to mention he was pretty easy on the eyes too. We dated for a few months, and naturally, I started to wonder if he was Mr. Right. I prayed and asked the Lord if this was the man He had for me, but I was unsure. Sometimes it is hard to see clearly when you are right in the midst of things.

One night, my boyfriend and I went out swing dancing. It was so much fun! It was a little place that gave an hour dance lesson beforehand, and then it was swing dancing until midnight! One of the things I liked most about the place was the opportunity to meet and dance with new people, not just the person you came with. There were all kinds of dancers afoot that night—young and old, short and tall, beginners and pros. We stayed until midnight, and then I went home and crashed.

The next morning, I woke up and began to pray and thank God for such a great time the previous night. I was reflecting on the evening and thinking about the different guys I danced with. One guy didn't know how to dance at all. He really wasn't much fun to dance with. Then there was another guy who knew the dance, but only that one basic move they taught us. It was the "rock-step spin"—spin being the key word. His grip was so tight that I couldn't break free, and because all he knew was the rock-step spin, the only thing we were doing was going in circles. I also thought about my boyfriend and how we danced together. He knew the dance, but it was a bit awkward when we were together. I could see his mind working as he thought about every move. While he was deciding on what to do next, I would decide I was bored and would try to do my own spins and dips. Most of the time, it didn't really work out. Needless to say, with two people trying to lead, we didn't dance very well together.

Finally, I remembered one guy that I danced with. He must have been swing dancing his entire life because he knew what he was doing. I knew the basic steps, but more importantly, he knew how to lead. His grip was sure but not too tight. He could turn my wrist to direct when I was to go out or spin, and he knew how to gently nudge my back to move in a new direction. All I could think of was "I'm not sure what I'm doing, but man, I look good!"

As I reflected on the night and smiled over all the fun we had, I clearly heard the Lord speak to my heart. He showed me a glimpse of each of the men I danced with and said, "This is a picture of what your marriage can be like." The first person I danced with did not know the dance at all. This person is someone who is not a Christian. He is not a believer in Christ and is therefore not one to even consider marrying.

Next was the guy who knew the dance but only knew the one move, "rock-step spin." This is a man who believes in Christ but has a very immature relationship with the Lord. He keeps fighting the same battles, circling around the same mountain over and over again. His lead is strong, but he will not take you where you want to go. With this type of man, you end up going around in circles, and you just get dizzy!

After that, I was reminded of my current boyfriend. We both knew the dance, but we were not quite in step with each other. It was a constant struggle of him being slow to decide and me wanting to take the lead. When two people are leading you will find that you don't really get anywhere, and both parties get frustrated. If I chose to stay in that relationship, I felt it would be a similar situation in marriage. I believe God said that I could marry this man if I wanted to. He was a good man, a Christian seeking after God, but we were not the best fit for each other. The Lord said I could marry him, but if I would wait, He had someone else in mind. This someone would be a perfect fit for me.

Then I recalled the last man that danced with me. He was fun, and it was so easy to dance with him. It was exciting and I never got bored. It was so natural to follow his lead that the thought never even crossed my mind to take the lead. That is what God said He has in store for me; someone who will take the lead as spiritual head of our household and lead with God's heart in mind. We would make each other look good. It would be comfortable, and we would be perfect for each other.

This is what I believe God has in mind for each of us. He has a perfect fit for who you are and the calling He has placed on your life. My friend, never settle for less than God's plan, God's best for your life. Psalm 84:11 says, "The Lord will withhold no good thing from those who do what is right" (NLT). He wants great things for you and will not withhold any good thing from you as you are seeking Him.

He wants good things for you and will not withhold all He desires for you as you are seeking Him.

STUDY GUIDE

ONCE UPON A TIME

After each chapter in this book, there will be a study guide with a few key points and some questions to help you reflect on where you are personally with the issues we discuss. I encourage you to take some time to answer the questions. Pray about them and when you answer, just be honest with yourself.

I have also added a section of "Fun Extras!" These are additional resources that I believe will be helpful on your journey. Some are books that dive deeper into the topics of that chapter, some are songs you can download online that will minister to you in this season, and some are just plain fun! Check them out!

Key Points:

- Never settle!

- There is no such thing as a perfect man, but I believe God has someone in mind that will be a perfect fit for each of us.

- God wants good things for you and will bring them into your life in His timing as you trust and seek Him.

My friend, never settle for less than God's plan, God's best for your life.

Personal Reflection:

1. What are your thoughts on marriage and "*The One*," the perfect fit for you? Do you believe there is one person for you, or do you think it's fine to marry anyone?

   _____

   _____

   _____

   _____

   _____

2. Do you think it matters who you marry? Why or why not?

   _____

   _____

   _____

   _____

   _____

Fun Extras!
A Man Worth Waiting For, book by Jackie Kendall
"Haven't Met You Yet," song by Michael Bublé

CHAPTER 2

SEEK AND FIND

"But seek first the kingdom of God and His righteousness,
and all these things shall be added to you"

Matthew 6:33 (NKJV).

When I was young, I loved doing Word Search Puzzles, some-times called "Seek And Finds." Although some people just scour the puzzle and look for any and all words that pop out, I found it was easiest to look for one word at a time. I would go to the first word, take the first letter, and then start at the top in search of that letter. Once I found the letter, it was easy to see the word that followed.

So how do you find what you're looking for? I think the key is making sure you are looking for the right thing and seeking that first and foremost. There is only One who will ever completely satisfy you, who loves you unconditionally, and who will never fail you. Are you in search of His heart?

Something I have seen throughout my life, and in the lives of many young men and women, is that often times God will not give us some of the things we desire because we put that so-called need in a place that only God was meant to fulfill. Sometimes we think, "If only I had this job… if only I were married… if only I had a family… if only…" You fill in the blank. The problem is that none of the things in this life will ultimately satisfy. God alone is meant to bring you love, peace, joy, and contentment. He does want to bless you with good things along the way, but He wants to have first place in your heart. He is well able to satisfy your deepest desires and your heart's cry, but you have to seek Him as your priority. When we seek after what we think we need more than we seek God, we find ourselves in a life full of disappointment, always looking for the next high.

What are you seeking after? God, your calling, a career, a spouse, a family? Whatever we desire most in our lives, pursuing above everything else, I believe we will find, although it may not end up as we imagined. For example, if a woman's top priority in life is to find a man and be married, she will most likely do just that. However, having a fruitful and lasting marriage is another thing entirely. If your goal is to be a successful business person and that is your main focus, you will probably be very successful in your area of expertise but at what expense, your health, family, or friends?

Our number one pursuit should be our relationship with our Father God. Matthew 6:33 says, "But seek first the kingdom of God and His righteousness, and all these things shall be added to you" (NKJV). When we seek God above everything else in life, He will add all the other things we need in His timing.

There are many desires in our hearts, and they are not necessarily wrong to have, but often we place those desires in a line with God. We seek them along with seeking God rather than making Him our priority. We shouldn't try to fit God into our lives. He should be the center of all we do. Jeremiah 29:12–13 says, "Then you will call on me and come and pray to me, and I will listen to you. You will seek me and find me when you seek me with all your heart" (NIV). A key word here is "ALL." The Message Version puts it this way, "When you get serious about finding Me and want it more than anything else, I'll make sure you won't be disappointed." When we search for many things, our attention is split and it's hard to find anything. When we search for one thing, our hunt will be much more successful, especially when that one thing is God.

God's Will For My Life

So how does this look practically? It means we don't fit God into our lives when it is convenient, but that we make Him the priority in our everyday lives. We put God at the center of our lives by reading the Bible, praying, and seeking His will for our lives, even for this day.

Have you ever wondered what the will of God is for your life? I know I have, but then I found it! Let me share it with you. In 1 Thessalonians 5:16–18, it says, "Rejoice always, pray without ceasing, and in everything give thanks; for this is the will of God in Christ Jesus for you" (NKJV). I know this doesn't give step-by-step instructions for who you should marry or what job you should take, but it does point us in the right direction for the path God would have us walk. Let's break it down.

"Rejoice always." This does not mean that you are happy all the time and that you walk around acting like nothing in this world goes wrong. That would be a bit delusional. What it does mean is resting in the joy of the Lord and the peace that He brings to every situation. We have a joy and hope like no other—God purchased our salvation so we could spend eternity with Him. If nothing else good ever happens in our lives, what Jesus did on the cross is enough. That should be a constant source of joy even in the darkest circumstances.

"Pray without ceasing." When I first heard this, I pictured an old man in a cloak walking around 24-7 with his head bowed and chanting. Let me assure you, that is not what God had in mind. I believe this scripture is to remind us that God is always here with us, and that we can be in constant communication with Him. Prayer at its most basic is simply talking with God. For me, it's like having a conversation with my best friend. Since my Friend is always there, it would be rude not to speak with Him. To pray without ceasing is to continually talk to God. Acknowledge His presence in your life, and thank Him for little things throughout the day. When you're having a rough go at it, tell Him. He knows and can give you the strength you need to finish strong.

"In everything give thanks." This does not mean that we have to be thankful for everything that comes our way because not everything in this world is good. To give thanks in everything means that we can see the best in every situation. We can choose to find the good in things. God said in Romans 8:28, "All things work together for good to those who love God, to those who are the called according to His purpose" (NKJV). Whatever happens in life, God will always be with you and see you through to the other side. When we set our eyes on Him, we can praise Him in good times and during tough times. It is usually in challenges that we grow the most.

"Rejoice always, pray without ceasing, and in everything give thanks; for this is the will of God in Christ Jesus for you."
1 Thessalonians 5:16–18 (NKJV)

Give It Up!

I remember several years ago when I wanted to move out of my parent's house. I looked for weeks trying to find a place that worked and that I could afford. I was so anxious to move that I wasn't trusting God to lead me to the right place. Finally one day, I gave up! I told God if I couldn't find a place, then He must want me to stay and I would stay until He opened the doors to leave. Very soon after that prayer, an old friend randomly texted me and asked if I might be interested in renting a house with her. She told me the cost and where we would be living, and I about did a backflip! I was so excited because it was better than anything I had looked at or imagined at less than half the cost.

That was just one instance, but there have been many times that I wanted something a bit much and held on too tightly to my supposed need. When this happens, usually God waits for me to give it up! There are things I wanted so much that I began seeking them even more than God. I was praying, but the focus of my prayers was on getting something I wanted and talking at God more than talking with God.

What are some things in your life that you want to have or situations that you wish to see changed? Do you HAVE TO have it? If there is anything or anyone in life you think, "I can't live without…," then we have a problem. That thing or that person is taking a place that only God should have in your heart. You need to recognize that only God can sustain you. He is the only one we can't live without.

But What If...

Let's get real for a moment. What would happen if you never get married? You may be sad sometimes and have some lonely days, but it's not the end of the world.

Would you turn your back on God or would you trust that He is still sovereign and He still loves you? Does it change your faith in God? Will you walk away because He doesn't always give you what you want? We need to choose God because He loves us and made a way for us to be with Him. If we can get to the point where we can honestly say in our hearts, "Lord, if I never get married, I will still serve You and love You with all my heart," life will be so much easier. I'm not saying this is an easy place to get to, but perhaps until we get to this point of being completely content and satisfied with God alone, we may not be ready for marriage.

You're Off The Hook!

Ladies, great news for you! Proverbs 18:22 says, "He who finds a wife finds a good thing, and obtains favor from the Lord" (NKJV). Did you catch that? Let's read it again. "HE who finds a WIFE." The Word says it right there—it's the man's job to find a wife, not the woman's job to find a husband. So, ladies, STOP LOOKING! This takes all of the pressure off of us as women to find the man God has for us. Proverbs 19:14 also states that "a prudent wife is from the Lord" (NIV). We are a gift from the Lord to be given to a man of His choosing. Seek after God and trust that if He wants us to meet Mr. Right then He will bring along the man in His timing and have our husbands find us!

STUDY GUIDE

SEEK AND FIND

Key Points:

- There is only One who will ever completely satisfy you, who loves you unconditionally, and who will never fail you.

- God wants to have first place in your heart.

- "Rejoice always, pray without ceasing, and in everything give thanks; for this is the will of God in Christ Jesus for you" 1 Thessalonians 5:16–18 (NKJV).

- "He who finds a wife finds a good thing, and obtains favor from the Lord" Proverbs 18:22 (NKJV). Stop searching for him—let him find you!

Personal Reflection:

1. Is there anything or anyone in your life that you believe you "can't live without?"

_____

_____

_____

_____

_____

2. If you never get married, will God be enough?

_____

_____

_____

_____

_____

3. What do you think God's will is for your life?

_____

_____

_____

_____

_____

Fun Extras!
"Keep Making Me," song by Sidewalk Prophets
"Seek Me," song by Watermark

_"Then you will call on me and come and pray to me,
and I will listen to you. You will seek me and find
me when you seek me with all your heart."_
Jeremiah 29:12–13 (NIV)

CHAPTER 3

NOT SO PRINCE CHARMING

I want to take a few moments to share about each of the men in our dance story from chapter 1. Chances are you have known some men that personify each of those and maybe have even dated some of them. By taking a closer look at what kind of man not to date, I believe it will be much easier to spot the real deal when he comes along.

Bachelor Number 1

Bachelor Number 1 is the man in our story who does not know the dance. In other words, this is the guy who is not a Christian. The Bible is pretty clear when it comes to marrying someone who doesn't believe in Jesus. In 2 Corinthians 6:14, it says, "Do not be unequally yoked together with unbelievers. For what fellowship has righteousness with lawlessness? And what communion has light with darkness?" (NKJV).

I like how the Message version translates the same verse in 2 Corinthians, "Don't become partners with those who reject God. How can you make a partnership out of right and wrong? That's not partnership; that's war." THAT'S WAR—strong words, but I believe there is a lot of truth in them. When a believer and an unbeliever marry, that is essentially what will happen, war. It's not necessarily a physical battle, but I guarantee you a spiritual battle will be taking place, and it will be fought for your future, your calling, and purpose.

Amos 3:3 says, "Can two people walk together without agreeing on the direction?" (NLT). If you marry someone who doesn't believe in Christ, you are committing and binding yourself to a man who is essentially going in a different direction than you. Your destination is heaven, and your journey should be to glorify God on the way. His journey, until he decides otherwise, is self-seeking and I'm sorry to say, toward hell. A relationship like this is usually either lonely (since they are still heading in different directions), short-lived (as they get frustrated with one another and give up) or filled with regret (as the Christian gives up the calling on her life in order to please a man).

Missionary Dating

Now perhaps you think I'm being too harsh when I say she's headed to heaven and he's headed to hell so they shouldn't be together. Maybe you have had the thought, "If I date him, I will be a positive influence in his life and can lead him to the Lord." Possible? Yes, but the greater likeliness is the reverse affect. When you date an unbeliever, you are already compromising your faith for a man. What this does is open you up to more compromise, and you become the one being influenced. What do you do when a guy says, "If you want to be with me you will…"? Where is the line?

The fact is, you've already crossed it. Let's dig a little deeper into this argument of dating a nonbeliever so you can be a positive influence. This sounds like a noble cause, but let me ask you this, why do you have to be dating this guy to be a positive influence? Yes, even Jesus hung around sinners and tax collectors, the down-and-out of His day, but there is a difference between being a witness and sharing a life together. Can you not be a witness to him as a friend or acquaintance?

I think if we get to the heart of the issue, most women who want to date a man who is not a Christian are doing it more so for their own benefit. It is nice to feel cherished and desired, and when the only men looking our way aren't Christians, we can start to make excuses for why it is okay that we go out with them.

Ladies, don't compromise your principles because you are lonely or feel like there are no good men out there. I promise you, there are godly men still out there, and you only need one! To have a man that is not a believer, you would either be leaving the "dance" to get him and walking away from the Lord, or you would be "dancing" to entice the guy to join you. The Bible tells us that there is no guarantee he will ever become a Christian. First Corinthians 7:16 speaks to someone married to an unbeliever, saying, "How do you know, wife, whether you will save your husband? Or, how do you know, husband, whether you will save your wife?" (NKJV). He may become a Christian, but he may not. To marry someone who doesn't believe in Christ would be compromising what God wants for you and no longer seeking His will first. According to the Bible, marrying an unbeliever should not be an option.

A Surrendered Life

There is another group of men that I think belong in this group. They are the ones who will say they are Christians but do not live a life that exemplifies a surrendering to Christ.

Though many may call themselves Christians, not all understand what it truly means to be a Christian—a follower of Christ. Christianity is not a religion but a relationship with Jesus. It is accepting God's love for us and then loving Him by living a life surrendered. Does the man you are interested in truly believe and follow Christ? It may take time to discern, but you will be able to tell if you really want to know. Who does he live for, himself or the Lord? We don't want to judge the person, but you can judge the fruit in a person's life as Matthew 7:16 says, "You will know them by their fruits" (NKJV).

To see the fruit in a person's life, you look at his character and the effects of his life. Is he kind? Does he follow through on what he says he will do? Does he speak with wisdom and encouragement or is he condescending and always putting others down? How is his reputation? These are some of the questions I would ask myself about a man I'm considering dating.

Bachelor Number 2

"Make sure there are no glaring weaknesses." Years ago, my pastor said this regarding the qualities of what a good leader should look like, and I believe the same should stand for your potential husband. I believe this statement sums up the problem with Bachelor Number 2. In my story, he was the man who knew the dance but only knew one move—the rock-step spin. I've defined this as the Christian man who believes in Jesus but keeps struggling with the same issues in his life. As the Israelites wandered in the desert forty years, going around the same old mountain, so does this man go around his mountain. This man may be a strong leader in your home, but he is not going in a direction that you want to follow.

One red flag could be the friends he hangs around. First Corinthians 15:33 says, "Bad company corrupts good character" (NIV). More often than not, we become like who we are with the most. Are the people he's around the most a positive or negative influence? Something else to be leery of is inconsistencies in his personality when he is around different people. Does he change depending on who he is with, or is he of good reputation no matter who he is around?

In my opinion, make him deal with his junk, any major baggage, before you forever commit yourself to carry it with him. I'm not talking about little issues, like he leaves the toilet seat up—that you may be able to work out together. What I am referring to is any deliberate sin in his life that continues to be a struggle. This issue may be a number of things. It could be an addiction to drugs or alcohol. He may have a problem with pornography. Maybe you are constantly catching him in a lie. Whatever the issue, it needs to be addressed before the I do's are said.

I promise you, there are godly men still out there, and you only need one!

Bachelor Number 3

Bachelor Number 3 can have many different faces, but it comes down to someone who is a Christian, an all-around pretty good guy but just not God's best for you.

We have to be careful not to let our hearts fall for a man simply because the gift of God on his life. The gifts and anointing are from the Lord, and Romans 11:29 says, "for God's gifts and His call are irrevocable" (NIV). Many people operate in the gifts that God has given them but don't live in a way that glorifies Him. I have been guilty of falling for a guy because of his position rather than simply because of who he is. I have always been drawn to guys in the ministry—pastors or worship leaders who are cute and seemingly on fire for the Lord. Just because we love the gifts in a man does not mean he is the man for us.

We also have to be careful that we don't try and make someone into the person we want them to be. I felt called to full-time ministry in the church, but the men I dated were not in ministry at that time. They were passionate about God and serving people, but I was a bit set in my thinking that I needed a man who would one day be in "full-time ministry." Well, in dating this obviously came up. The first guy said his dad was a pastor so maybe he would be one day, who knows! He was trying to fit into my mold, and I was trying to make him fit. That's not fair at all! You can't change a person, nor should we try. We need to love the man God gives us, not the position a man holds or may hold in the future. Positions change, seasons will come and go, but the people stay the same. If he's the right guy, know the person and choose to love him for who he is.

In my story, God spoke to me specifically about the man I was dating, my Bachelor Number 3. As we were literally on the dance floor, I was getting bored with the basic steps and wanted to do something different. Several times during the dance, I tried to take the lead and add a spin or a dip. As you can imagine, it didn't work out very well. Only one person can lead in a dance—try it if you don't believe me. We were both trying to lead, and the only thing we succeeded in doing was frustrating one another. The Lord told me that this was what my marriage would be like if I decided to be with him, frustrating. It would be hard for me to follow, and I would constantly be fighting to take the lead from my husband. That could be in part because the man hasn't learned to be a leader or could be because the woman hasn't learned to submit.

As He spoke to me about my Bachelor Number 3, the Lord showed me that submitting to our husbands and letting them be the leaders of our households is a good thing. It's how He created it to be.

Submission...Dun, Dun, Duuuuuun!

If you are like most ladies I know, you hear the word "submit" and you don't get the best feelings inside. I used to hate that word and even wanted to stick my chin up a bit, getting a little indignant. "I am a competent adult who doesn't need to be told what I can or cannot do."

Ephesians 5:22 states, "Wives, submit to your own husbands, as to the Lord. For the husband is head of the wife, as also Christ is head of the church" (NKJV).

As the wife in a godly marriage, you are essentially giving up some freedom you had in the past and have to trust your husband to make wise decisions. You are no longer the final say but have a partner in the decision making process. You can look at this in two lights, but I would opt that the good outweighs the bad. Having someone help with decisions means you have someone to help carry the weight of those decisions, the responsibilities, and the consequences. You are partners in this, but if there is a disagreement on a decision and it is nothing that goes against the Word of God, then I believe the final decision should go to your husband as head of the house. That doesn't mean he has ultimate control and you have no say, but it does leave the final say to him. Now a wise man will discuss issues with his wife and receive input, for there is safety in counsel, but ultimately, the decision rests on him. This is just one reason it is so important to trust the man you marry to seek and hear from God.

How Is This A Bad Plan?

Bachelor Number 3 in my story can be a very large range of men. Your Bachelor Number 3 could be a wonderful, handsome, godly man, but if he isn't God's best for you, the man God would have you to be with, then he's the wrong man for you. This is often the hardest to discern and even harder to let go. "I like him, he likes me, and we both love You. How is this a bad plan, God?" As He told me, it is not bad, it's just not the best. I chose to wait a while longer and believe God's best is yet to come. He has a plan. Let's trust Him together.

STUDY GUIDE

NOT SO PRINCE CHARMING

Key Points:

- Do not compromise your faith by dating a man who doesn't believe in Christ.

- Christianity is not a religion, but a relationship with Jesus. It is accepting God's love for us and then loving Him by living a life surrendered.

- Beware of any glaring weaknesses in the men you date.

- Just because we love the gifts in a man, does not mean he is the man for us.

- When you are dating, think about your ability to submit to that man's leadership should you decide to marry—and remember, submit is not a bad word!

"Don't become partners with those who reject God. How can you make a partnership out of right and wrong? That's not partnership; that's war…"
2 Corinthians 6:14 (The Message)

Personal Reflection:

1. What are your thoughts on dating an unbeliever to win him to Christ?

_____
_____
_____
_____
_____

2. Do you believe you live a surrendered life to God? If not, how could you start?

_____
_____
_____
_____
_____

3. How do you feel about submitting to your future husband?

_____
_____
_____
_____
_____

Fun Extras!
"I Will Wait For You" by Official P4CM Poet
Janette…IKZ, YouTube video
"Have You Seen This Man?" song by Amanda Wilders

---- CHAPTER 4 ----

MR. RIGHT FOR YOU

So now that we have seen what Mr. Wrong looks like, let's take a minute to look at Mr. Right. Is there such a man—someone who can do no wrong, the perfect man with no faults, great faith, and an amazing body? Nope, he doesn't exist! Well, like I said, there is no perfect man, but I believe there is a perfect fit for you and for me!

How Do You Recognize Him?

Look at your track record. What kind of men are you attracting? What do the men you have dated have in common? I encourage you to think about the type of man that you want to marry. Is this close to the type of men you have dated in the past? Do you even know what kind of man you want to marry? If you have never stopped to really think about it and just know you want a "great guy," that may be part of the problem.

I want to challenge you to set some time aside with a pen and paper and write down everything you can think of that you desire in a husband. Be as detailed as you want to be, but before you begin, separate your list into two columns—Priorities and Preferences. I'll get you started at the study guide following this chapter.

Your priorities are going to be the things that are non-negotiable. They are the things that you will not settle for less than. If a man does not have these, then I would not even consider dating him. The number 1 on our list should be that he is a Christian. Maybe that's all on this list. I have a few others such as I won't marry a man who is an alcoholic or a man who smokes. What are yours?

Your preferences are going to be everything else, anything that you would like in a husband. Yep, write it all—dark hair, blue eyes, a good sense of humor, maybe even a man who cooks! What would your perfect guy look like? Now keep in mind that this is a PREFERENCE list. It doesn't necessarily mean that when the right man comes along he will match everything on your list.

"Why even make the list then?" you ask. For one thing, it helps you to recognize the type of men you are attracted to and see if anything is misaligned. I also think it will be fun to look back on when we are married and see what we dreamed up versus who God has for us. I have this hunch that what God has in store is so much better than anything we could come up with. I have also heard from several ladies who did this, and they were amazed how God gave them EVERYTHING they had on their lists (even the silly things) and so much more. Who knows what the future holds!

As you are creating this list, don't forget to stop and ask the opinion of the One who matters most. Pray and ask the Lord what kind of man He sees as worthy to have your hand and your heart.

Don't Do It Alone

I think something very important to remember when choosing the right person to be with is not to make the decision alone. Yes, ultimately the decision is yours to make, but as Proverbs 11:14 says, "In the multitude of counselors there is safety" (NKJV). I wouldn't ask anyone and everyone their opinion on your relationships but go to people who are spiritually mature that you trust. Ask the hard questions from those who have seen you two together over a period of time. "Am I a better person when I'm with him?" "Is there anything amiss in our relationship that maybe I am not seeing?" Ask family and friends their opinion and be ready to hear with an open mind. They have your best interest at heart.

Another thing, don't keep the guy a secret or locked away from family and friends. It can be detrimental to isolate yourselves from the world. I understand not wanting to scare the guy off with family right away, but they have to meet eventually. If you're afraid of being disillusioned to this perfect man, you need to just rip the Band-Aid off—he's not perfect, and sometimes family can help you see it, which is in fact a good thing. They will often see a much clearer picture of the man you are with. They don't wear those "rose-colored glasses" that you may have put on. Take what they say, think it over, and pray about it. Then you decide what the next move is.

Good, Acceptable, Or Perfect?

I told you that I believe God has a man in mind who will be a perfect fit for each of us. I want to take a moment to elaborate on this. By making this statement, I am not necessarily saying that there is only one person out there for you, your soul mate, and if you don't find him, your life will be miserable the rest of your days. If there was only one person in the world for us, what happens if someone else marries my person!?! I think there are people who suit us best, suit our personalities and callings, some better than the others. I just believe that God knows who would be the very best fit and is willing to share that with us if we ask… and wait.

Romans 12:2 talks about the good, perfect, and acceptable will of God. I think often women grow tired of waiting and settle for good or acceptable. There are probably many that would be good for us and many more who are acceptable—any man who is a Christian, I would imagine. Don't settle. Ask God when a man comes along, "Is this your best for my life and for his?"

How do we know the perfect will of God? Let's look at the entirety of the above verse in Romans 12:2, "And do not be conformed to this world, but be transformed by the renewing of your mind, that you may prove what is that good and acceptable and perfect will of God" (NKJV). The best way to renew our minds is through reading the Word of God and spending time with Him on a regular basis. Reading the Bible allows us to know Him better. We are reading His words to us and learning His heart. Pray. Talk to Him and know Him better.

Ultimately, I know we serve a God who is bigger than we can possibly imagine, and His ways are far above our ways. I don't pretend to know everything, but I know that God is sovereign. He knows us inside and out, past and future, good, bad, and ugly. He knows the type of man that would complement our strengths and weaknesses, who would click with our personality, who has similar passions, and who feels called in the same direction as we feel called. God knows who would suit us best.

All The Single Guys

Have you ever been in a place where you find yourself looking at every single guy that comes across your path and asking yourself, "Could this be the one?" I admittedly was in such a state of mind not long ago. I went to a Christian Bible college where the vast majority of students were single young adults. Where better to find a future husband, right? Possibly, but that should not be the focus—obviously.

Before I left home, there were many jokes about meeting Mr. Right, and I did wonder if I might just meet him there. The first few weeks at Bible college, I had a hard time not looking at every guy and assessing him as a potential Mr. Right. There were also a lot of jokes about the first semester students and the "six month rule." No dating the first six months! That was a great rule to keep us better focused on our studies. As I and other first-semester ladies endeavored to focus on our studies, we had some well-needed chats about why we were there. I had a great conversation with a girlfriend of mine and saw how silly my thinking had gotten. God led me halfway around the world to a Christian college to draw me closer to Him. God was the reason I attended the college, and I realized that if I continued to keep my mind set on God first, there was no way He would let me miss the man he had for me if he was there.

There's another thing I felt like the Lord spoke to me recently that I want to share with you. It is simple, but I had not realized it before. The Lord showed me three qualities that my husband will have that no other men thus far in my life have had:

1. He will have godly character.

2. He will be attracted to me and pursue me.

3. I will be attracted to him.

These are three simple things, but I realized that no man who has come across my path has completely had all three of these. Lots of men have met two, but they are not the men for me. When I come across a man who meets all three of these things, then I may want to take a second look. How about you?

How Do You Know?

Will God tell me if the man I'm dating is my husband? Yes, but probably in more subtle ways than you would like. It will likely take time to discern. Colossians 3:15 says, "And let the peace of God rule in your hearts" (NKJV). Another version talks about peace being your "umpire." Let peace make the final call on important decisions. You will know peace because in your heart you will have a sense of right, an internal calmness about the decision. A lack of peace means there is a check, a sense to hold back before moving forward. Be sure to give yourself enough time to discern true peace. Sometimes the newness and excitement of a relationship can be misleading and give you a false sense of peace. Use wisdom and allow the Holy Spirit to guide you.

I like how Jackie Kendall put it in her book, *A Man Worth Waiting For.*

> One day our daughter was wondering the same thing: how would she know which guy was the best for her? I told her that God's best for her would always complement the direction God wanted her to go. In other words, he would have goals similar to hers.

> The single life is like a big running track with all these freshly painted lanes. One day she will be running in her lane, relentlessly in pursuit of Jesus, looking ahead

and not around, when all of a sudden she will hear this someone approaching.

If this someone is her Boaz, she will not have to stop running, she will not have to change her pace, and she won't have to look behind her, because before she knows it, he will be running alongside her. He will keep up with her, and they will continue the race at a complementary pace. This will be her running partner for the journey ahead. They will encourage each other and not trip each other.

Remember to be patient in anticipation of one coming alongside you, who will be panting in relentless pursuit of Jesus.[1]

"I've got my eye on the goal, where God is beckoning us onward—to Jesus. I'm off and running, and I'm not turning back."
Ephesians 3:14 (The Message)

I LOVE IT! The Bible says something similar. Paul says it in Philippians 3:14–4:1.

Friends, don't get me wrong: By no means do I count myself an expert in all of this, but I've got my eye on the goal, where God is beckoning us onward—to Jesus.

I'm off and running, and I'm not turning back. So let's keep focused on that goal, those of us who want everything God has for us. If any of you have something else in mind, something less than total commitment, God will clear your blurred vision—you'll see it yet! Now that we're on the right track, let's stay on it.

Stick with me, friends. Keep track of those you see running this same course, headed for this same goal. There are many out there taking other paths, choosing other goals, and trying to get you to go along with them. I've warned you of them many times; sadly, I'm having to do it again. All they want is easy street. They hate Christ's Cross. But easy street is a dead-end street. Those who live there make their bellies their gods; belches are their praise; all they can think of is their appetites.

But there's far more to life for us. We're citizens of high heaven! We're waiting the arrival of the Savior, the Master, Jesus Christ, who will transform our earthy bodies into glorious bodies like His own. He'll make us beautiful and whole with the same powerful skill by which He is putting everything as it should be, under and around Him.

My dear, dear friends! I love you so much. I do want the very best for you. You make me feel such joy, fill me with such pride. Don't waver. Stay on track, steady in God. (The Message)

Paul said it, but I will say it again to you. My friend, I truly want the very best for you and so does God. Don't waver. Stay on track. Be steadfast in God.

STUDY GUIDE

MR. RIGHT FOR YOU

Key Points:

- I believe that God knows the man who would be the very best fit for you and is willing to share that information if you are willing to ask, listen, and usually (and unfortunately) wait.

- It is important to have accountability and not make important decisions alone. The ultimate decision is yours, but it is wise to seek advice from those you trust who have your best interest at heart. Others may see what you can't because they aren't as close to the situation.

- The best way to renew our minds is through reading the Word of God and spending time with Him on a regular basis. Pray—talk with the Lord and get to know Him better. You'll be surprised at what He speaks to your heart.

- Let peace make the final call on important decisions.

"In the multitude of counselors there is safety."
Proverbs 11:14 (NKJV)

Personal Reflection:

1. Write the top 5 things you remember about the last 2 men you dated. If you haven't dated, write the top 5 things you remember about a guy you liked in the past. I'm sure there's at least one!

Man 1:   Man 2:

_____   _____

_____   _____

_____   _____

_____   _____

_____   _____

2. Do the above qualities reflect the type of man you one day hope to marry? Are they qualities you must have or are they superficial?

_____

_____

_____

_____

_____

3. Think about a time when you made a tough decision. How did you decide what the right decision was? Did you have peace with that decision?

_____

_____

_____

_____

_____

Fun Extras!
"6'2," song by Marie Miller
"Soar," song by Meredith Andrews

My Challenge to You:

Make a list of everything you could ever want in the perfect guy. What does your Mr. Right look like? Get as detailed as you want— brown hair, blue eyes, loves to cook, not a Cubs fan, I don't know, whatever you want! When creating your list, use the columns below and determine if the things you desire are preferences or priorities. Preferences are the silly little things that would be nice to have but aren't necessarily deal breakers. Priorities are the non-negotiables, the things that you will not bend on. Pray about these and see how those you've dated (or will date) hold up. Don't settle on someone who doesn't make the priority list!

Priorities (Non-negotiables)   Preferences

_____   _____

_____   _____

_____   _____

_____   _____

_____   _____

_____   _____

_____   _____

_____   _____

_____   _____

_____   _____

_____   _____

_____   _____

_____   _____

_____   _____

_____   _____

_____   _____

_____   _____

Priorities (Non-negotiables)   Preferences

_____   _____

_____   _____

_____   _____

_____   _____

_____   _____

_____   _____

_____   _____

_____   _____

_____   _____

_____   _____

_____   _____

_____   _____

_____   _____

_____   _____

_____   _____

_____   _____

_____   _____

_____   _____

_____   _____

_____   _____

_____   _____

_____   _____

_____   _____

_____   _____

_____   _____

_____   _____

CHAPTER 5

THE DATING GAME

Why, When, How?

Now that we have answered the question of who to date, let's talk briefly about the why, when, and how we should date. Some see dating as a social norm. Everyone who is single is supposed to be dating, right? It's nice to have someone to go out with on those lonely days. It's the fun, cool thing to do, and the dating age seems to be starting younger and younger. I've even heard elementary school girls talking about their boyfriends. I personally decided to break the mold and went in a different direction.

When I was fifteen, I had a young man ask me out. He was a nice enough guy, but I didn't answer him right away. When I prayed about it, I decided I didn't want to date until I was ready to get married. The way I see it, the godly reason we date is that it would lead to possibly getting married. At fifteen, I was not old enough nor was I nearly ready to get married so that was my answer. Any dating that is not in the hopes of marriage or for the purpose of possibly getting married can only lead to temptation and places God has said we should not go. This is my opinion, but it is something I feel the Lord has directed me in, and I believe it can be a help to you.

Call me old-fashioned, but I highly suggest getting to know each other as friends for a while before dating. I also suggest hanging out with a group of friends rather than getting to know a guy on your own. When with a group of friends, we tend to be more relaxed, more ourselves rather than put on our best face for a date. Having a foundation of friendship with a man long before you date him will save you a lot of heartbreak. If you are content with where you are in life and are patient, it is not difficult to see who a man is simply by watching him in a group setting. Who are his friends? How is his character? Does he make God and church a priority in his life? In the last chapter, we made a list of our non-negotiables. You have determined what the man God has in mind for you looks like, so watch and don't settle for less.

True To Yourself

There needs to be a distinction between putting on your best face while you're dating versus putting on a false face. After the last man I dated, I looked back and realized that I was trying so hard to do the right thing that I wasn't 100 percent true to who I am. What do I mean? Quite often, I would think something but be afraid it was the wrong thing to say so I would simply stay quiet. So the man I dated may have thought I was a sweet, quiet young lady when in reality I was kind of obnoxious and a bit of a sarcastic little thing. I was so caught up in being the best me I could be that I didn't show the whole me. I realized this after we were hanging out and just goofing off a bit. He looked at me with almost amazed eyes and said, "Wow, you're really fun!" Now, I am sure he meant that as a compliment, but I was thinking, "Of course, I'm fun! I'm Amanda! How long have we been dating?" I saw that he was attracted to the sweet, godly woman (that I obviously am ☺), but as important as that is, there is a lot more that makes up me.

Along those lines, you need to be careful not to change who you are as far as the activities, music, and foods you like too. You don't have to like what he likes to make him like you… Tongue twister, ha! If you do, he's not the guy for you! You may think you're just taking an interest in what he likes, but there is a fine line between taking an interest and basically lying to make yourself fit into his world. Later you may feel you have to fight to regain your identity. I have heard from married women who started out that way, and eventually, they became resentful because they always did what their husbands wanted. Or on the flip side, they get married and their husbands find a totally different woman who doesn't like to fish or bowl or watch football or whatever with them anymore. Don't compromise who you are to try and win someone's heart or for fear that they will reject you. If they reject you, it may hurt initially, but ultimately, they are not the best man for you, and it will hurt a lot less to find out now. It is, of course, very important to take your time when deciding who you will spend the rest of your life with. Get to a place where pretenses drop and you both get to see the good, the bad, and the ugly of each other. Better now than after the "I do's" are said.

Dirty Laundry

When you are in a serious relationship, there needs to be at least one very honest conversation concerning any "dirty laundry." There are most likely things about yourself that you don't share with many people. This could be something you've done in the past, something that's happened to you, or maybe a bad habit that still tempts you.

If there is something you are afraid to tell because you think he might leave you, it is most definitely something that needs to get out in the open eventually. If this is a man you want to spend the rest of your life with, he should be a man that you can trust and who will love you no matter what. We don't want to hide something and have it come out later. I don't want my husband to feel I tricked him into marrying me by hiding part of who I was. Frankly, we wouldn't want any of those types of surprises after we get married and neither would they.

This is a big step in any relationship. Don't rush into this step but don't avoid it either. When you are seriously considering marriage to this man, it's time to talk. This probably won't be easy. It requires the ability to be vulnerable with each other. It's possible that someone will get hurt, but it's necessary to move forward. Share your heart and be ready to hear his. You may be surprised at what you hear as well. Be compassionate and understanding. Most importantly, after you leave the conversation, agree to be in prayer over what you've shared and heard. Ask the Lord to help you with it and move forward as the Lord gives you peace and direction.

Fight Vs. Conflict

While I was dating, I began to think ahead about marriage and had a personal revelation that I would like to share with you. I started to think about how disagreements would of course come and how much I hated the fighting some spouses have. I asked the Lord how a healthy marriage should look—how a Christian couple should fight. Then the Lord showed me a new way to look at it. He said that in a marriage (or in any relationships for that matter), when disagreements arise, you should not think of them as fights to be won but conflicts to be resolved. A fight implies two opposing sides, each one with a desire to be victor over the other, and usually, someone gets hurt. A conflict, however, is when two or more people are working together to find a solution. The people don't always necessarily agree, but they are on the same side, and they will work things out through communication and maybe even some compromise.

How do you react when disagreements come in a dating relationship? Maybe you aren't in a dating relationship right now, but what about in your work environments, teams you are a part of, or family relations? If your first instinct is to go into battle mode, then I think it's time to reevaluate. Prepare now and save yourself the pain of working it out later. Resolve not to take up arms when a disagreement comes but to step back and work out the issue without hurting someone. After all, you're not enemies!

Red Alert!

Red flag when dating: a man asks you out but wants you to pay your own way. I haven't had many boyfriends, but this has happened to me with two different guys! You would think after the first time I would have learned my lesson, but I was just as enamored with the second guy, and I let it slide. Ladies, if a man asks you out, assuming we've moved passed the friend zone, it is my strong opinion that he should flip the bill. You may think I'm being an old-fashioned snob, but I disagree. A true gentleman knows how to treat a lady!

Look at this story in the Bible. Matthew 13:44–46 says, "The Kingdom of Heaven is like a treasure that a man discovered hidden in a field. In his excitement, he hid it again and sold everything he owned to get enough money to buy the field. Again, the Kingdom of Heaven is like a merchant on the lookout for choice pearls. When he discovered a pearl of great value, he sold everything he owned and bought it!" (NLT). When a wise man discovers a rare treasure, he will sell all he has to lay hold of it! You should have a man who sees you as a treasure, a treasure worth investing in.

My friend, you are worth far more than earthly treasure, and you deserve a man who sees that. A man worthy of your heart will see his time with you and the money he spends on you as the best investment he will ever make. You may not care about paying for your own meal or maybe even his, but don't just think about today. Look at the long-term repercussions. If he is stingy in the beginning, he'll be stingy to the end. And if the man who asks you out can't afford to pay for a meal, then he most definitely cannot afford a wife. Matthew 6:21 says, "For where your treasure is, there your heart will be also" (NIV). Is at least part of his heart with you?

God Told Me

If someone says to you, "God told me you're my wife," run for the hills! Well, at least be very cautious and I speak from experience. For the few males who might have picked up this book in order to gain some insight and to better understand the single, female psyche, good luck to you! Here is a word of advice, if you really do feel God is telling you that this is the one, do yourself and the gal a favor and keep it to yourself. First off, we are all human and sometimes we think we hear from God when maybe it's just the pizza we ate the night before or wishful thinking. Secondly, if you did hear from God, that's awesome! Keep it to yourself until after the "I do's" have been said. God spoke to give you direction and confirmation. He is more than capable of speaking to your counterpart in His timing.

And ladies, the same goes for you. If you feel like God is telling you that Bobbie Blue Eyes is your husband, pray about it and let God tell Mr. Right. There probably aren't too many better ways to scare off a guy than to tell him you're going to marry him! Think of it this way. By telling someone, "God told me such and such," you are leaving no room for error or argument. If God said it, then it has to be true, right? Yes, if God really said it. By telling someone, "God told me," you are conveying something as a fact without the possibility of you missing it. You are in effect backing the other person into a corner and putting pressure on them to agree with you. Saying this shows pride that you heard from God when the other person didn't and can also add unnecessary confusion if the other person hasn't heard that from the Lord.

Someone once told me, "God said you're my wife." At the time, he really believed it too. I was still unsure about our relationship, and when he said that, it left me feeling a bit anxious. Don't get me wrong, I was flattered to hear that I was "everything he had ever prayed for in a wife," but telling me, "God said," made me feel like the decision was made rather than God speaking to me. Ironically enough, he broke up with me just weeks later. Did God change His mind? Maybe we just get caught up in emotions sometimes instead of waiting on the Lord.

If someone says to you, "God told me you're my wife,"
run for the hills! Well, at least be very cautious.

A New Equation

I know early on in your education that a math teacher probably taught you a few basic equations such as $1 + 1 = 2$ and $1/2 + 1/2 = 1$. I'm here to tell you that in life and in marriage, these equations do not add up! Our new equation will be $1 + 1 + 1 = 1$, the ONE (God) + the one whole ME + the someday one whole HUSBAND = one COMPLETE (Lacking Nothing) Marriage.

It is a common misconception that we should be on this hunt for our other half, a spouse who will make us whole. I know in math one-half plus one-half equals one whole, but I can assure you the same is not true when it comes to marriage or any relationship for that matter. One-half plus one-half does not make a whole in marriage—it makes a mess. Two halves in a marriage consist of each person believing the other should make them complete, always taking and never satisfied.

We all love the popular movie scene where Tom Cruise rushes in and tells Renée Zellweger that "you complete me," but unlike what movies portray, we are not made to complete each other. Only God can complete us. We are made to complement rather than complete one another.

No other relationship is able to fulfill and satisfy you like your relationship with God. He is the only One who can fill the voids in your heart. Nothing and no one else was ever meant to do that. You have to be complete and content with God, as a single, before you can be complete as a couple. Half a man and half a woman do not make a whole marriage!

When two whole people marry, they are already satisfied by God Himself and can look to give unselfishly to their spouse rather than take. Before you marry, God wants you to be made whole in Him. Know that God alone can satisfy. Know who you are and who He created you to be. You are a daughter of the King and every good and perfect gift comes from God—not from your husband.

The Test Of True Love

Here's a little test I learned in elementary school that might give you a clue to if this is the right man for you. It's called TRUE LOVE. Write your name and his name on a piece of paper. Then add up the amount of letters in each of your names that are in true love like so:

Amanda Wilders + Zac Efron

T - 0	L - 1
R - 2	O -1
U - 0	V - 0
E - 2	E - 2
4	4 = 44

Scoring:

0–25	Definitely Not
26–50	Not Likely
51–75	There's a Chance
76–100	Looking Good
100+	TRUE LOVE!

Unfortunately things don't look good for me and Zac, ha! Okay, obviously there is no formula or real test that can find your true love, but a good test of a relationship is the test of time. Don't rush into anything. The longer you get to know a person, the more you know about the person—that's just a plain and simple fact. In the beginning stages of infatuation, you may feel so in love that the person can do no wrong. "Flaws, what flaws? My guy is perfect!" New is exciting but ask any married person, and they will reassure you that your dream guy has issues just like the rest. Hang out for a while and see if these issues are things you can live with for the rest of your life. Take enough time that you don't have to find them out after you get married.

Another part of the test of time is how you handle separation from each other. Is it out of sight, out of mind? If you don't really think about the person when he's gone, it's probably a sign that it's time to move on. If you miss the person, I'd say you may be on the right track.

STUDY GUIDE

THE DATING GAME

Key Points:

- There needs to be a distinction between putting on your best face while you're dating versus putting on a false face. Don't be someone you're not to win a guy.

- When you are in a serious relationship, there needs to be at least one very honest conversation concerning any "dirty laundry."

- It is a common misconception that we should be on this hunt for our other half, a spouse who will make us whole. God is the only one who can completely satisfy and fill the emptiness we feel at times. You have to be complete and content with God, as a single, before you can be complete as a couple. Half a man and half a woman does not a whole marriage make!

Before you marry, God wants you to be made whole in Him. Know that God alone can satisfy.

Personal Reflection:

1. Why do you date or want to date? (Examples: Fun, loneliness, peer pressure, hopes of marriage, etc.)

   _____

   _____

   _____

   _____

   _____

2. If you are currently in a relationship, is there anything you don't want to tell your boyfriend for fear that he will leave you? Yes_____ No_____

   If yes, pray about this issue. If your relationship is serious, decide if and when you need to share it.

3. Think about a time when you put on your "best face" to impress— this could be for a guy, new friends, a potential employer, or anyone. Do you feel you were still true to yourself, or did you project a false identity to be what you think they wanted?

   _____

   _____

   _____

   _____

   _____

4. When you think about the last person you had a big fight with, were you trying to win a battle or were you trying to resolve a conflict? How could you have handled it better?

_____

_____

_____

_____

_____

5. Because you know you want to:
   Your Name:_____
   His Name:_____

T - ___	L - ___
R - ___	O - ___
U - ___	V - ___
E - ___	E - ___

   _____

   ____   ____   =____

0–25	Definitely Not
26–50	Not Likely
51–75	There's a Chance
76–100	Looking Good
100+	TRUE LOVE!

Fun Extras!
"Try," song by Colbie Caillat

CHAPTER 6

EN GARDE!

An interesting twist on the story! In the middle of writing this book, I found myself in a relationship with a kind, godly gentleman, and I wondered if he might be "the one." As you may have gathered, I do not date often and only consider dating a man if I think he may be the man I will marry. He would have to be a friend, first and foremost, and through that friendship, I would hope to see his values and the characteristics I believe will be in my husband. He was just such a man, jealous much?

I was praying throughout the relationship and asking God if he was the man for me, but I never heard a yes or a no. I had peace as we dated and never felt I should break up with him. Looking back now, I honestly believe the answer from God was no, but I think He had a few things to teach me through the relationship. You see, I have only had two boyfriends in my life. I broke up with the first one, but this one—this kind, amazing man of God—broke up with me. Being dumped sucks! Can I say that in a book LOL? Well, for those who have experienced it, you would say the same thing I'm sure. I do not regret the experience though because I have a whole new "chapter in my book" and a whole new group of ladies now that can relate to my story.

Breaking Up

Have you ever stopped to think about the term "break up?" Let's look at that word, break, for a moment. The dictionary defines break as:

> to smash, split, or divide into parts violently; reduce
> to pieces or fragments
> to infringe, ignore, or act contrary to
> to dissolve or annul
> to lacerate; wound[2]

OUCH! Now, I don't know about you, but when I read these, all I see is my heart getting viciously smashed into pieces by a man. BREAK UP. What a terrible concept! I know that, for the most part, we don't mean it to be this way. When we break up with somebody, we usually want to spare the other person's feelings. "It's not you, it's me." All the same, the result of a break up often does leave someone shattered in pieces.

It is not fun to be on the raw end of a break up, but I came out on the other side with little more than a flesh wound. So what is a flesh wound and how do we get through a break up with only that?

The dictionary defines it as "a wound that does not penetrate beyond the flesh; a slight or superficial wound[3]." It is something that hurts in the moment but does not leave a lasting scar. I am grateful to God for the advice I was given years ago that has kept me from much heartache and pain, and this advice I give to you, "Guard your heart."

"Guard your heart above all else, for it determines the course of your life."

Proverbs 4:23 (NLT)

Guard Your Heart

Right before I started dating my first boyfriend, I received a word of wisdom from a wonderful lady in my church. (Thank you, Miss Nancy!) She felt like the Lord wanted to simply say, "Guard your heart." I didn't really understand what that meant, especially never having dated before. After a few months of dating, however, I started to realize the meaning behind those words. The more time you spend with someone, the more drawn you are to them. You can easily give your heart away to someone whom the Lord never intended it for.

To guard your heart, you also need to be careful how much you share with someone as well as how much stock you take in their opinions. The more you share about yourself, especially things that not many know, the more vulnerable you are. Opening your heart to a man in this way could form a connection that may not be wise if this man is not ultimately yours. It can also allow for opinions and criticism into your personal life that can affect you negatively.

For me, guarding my heart meant taking things slowly. Pulling back a bit when I was unsure if the relationship should move forward. I never had complete peace that the man I was dating was my husband, so I didn't allow my heart and mind to think of him as such. Proverbs 4:23 says, "Guard your heart above all else, for it determines the course of your life" (NLT). This is so true. If you let your heart fall for a man that is not right for you, the entire direction of your life could be altered.

On Guard!

You not only need to guard your heart, but you also need to guard your mind and body. Protect your body by the way you treat it. What you do to it and put on it is a representation of Christ and influences how you are looked at. "Don't you realize that your body is the temple of the Holy Spirit, who lives in you and was given to you by God? You do not belong to yourself, for God bought you with a high price. So you must honor God with your body" 1 Corinthians 6:19–20 (NIV). Be modest in what you wear. We don't want to cause our brothers in Christ to stumble. I understand that it is nice to have someone view us as beautiful, but God has called us to be beautiful on the inside which radiates outward. Causing men to lust by wearing low-cut shirts and tight jeans is not what God intended. Matthew 5:27–28 says, "You have heard that it was said, 'You shall not commit adultery.' But I tell you that anyone who looks at a woman lustfully has already committed adultery with her in his heart" (NIV). Do you want someone sinning because of what you wear? Do you really want them thinking about you in that way?

Let's look at the flip side as well. How do you look at men? The scripture above is most often associated with the way men look at women, but I assure you that we are not immune from that. Do you see a guy jogging down the street and spend a little too much time looking at his six-pack abs? Take control of your mind and keep your eyes on the road, ha! The world may say what's the harm in looking, but it often says what's the harm in touching too. We are called to a higher standard of living. The scripture says in Romans 12:2, "Do not conform to the pattern of this world, but be transformed by the renewing of your mind" (NIV). One way to renew our minds is stated in Philippians 4:8. It says, "Whatever is true, whatever is noble, whatever is right, whatever is pure, whatever is lovely, whatever is admirable—if anything is excellent or praiseworthy—think about such things" (NIV). Let's keep our minds on what matters most.

Boundaries

Ladies, I cannot stress enough the importance of setting boundaries. Whether or not you currently have a boyfriend, I challenge you today to make a list of boundaries for any relationship with guys. Be specific. Before you ever step foot into the situation, you need to know your boundaries. If boundaries aren't previously set, you won't know when the line is crossed until it's too late.

It is essential to communicate your boundaries early on in a dating relationship. It may feel awkward talking about it, but trust me, it will be easier to talk about boundaries before you enter a situation than when you are about to cross them. Honesty upfront is the best way to go. If he doesn't respect your boundaries early on, then he is not the guy for you. Find out early and move on!

Here are a few boundary decisions I believe all of us should make ahead of time. To kiss or not to kiss, that is the question. Another couple questions would be about touching, sex, how much time to spend together, time spent alone, and the "L" word (Love).

Would you like to know a few of my boundaries? Of course you would! Let's see… Hugs, yes. Kisses, not without a ring. Touching—hands yes, legs not so much. Sex, no way Jose. Time alone—yes, but in public places. Love—I just won't say it until I'm sure. My advice is to think about how you would respond to someone telling you "I love you" ahead of time. Don't feel pressured into answering in kind. Thanks is always cute and acceptable if you just aren't sure. Now, I'm a bit more strict with my boundaries than you may be, but these are the things that I've prayed about and believe are best for me.

Not only should you set boundaries, but you also need to think ahead about how to keep those boundaries in place. For example, if you desire to avoid sex before marriage, a good idea would be not to put yourself in a situation where you may be tempted. A personal boundary I set for myself is that I will not be alone in a house with a man—friend, boyfriend, or even fiancé. My reason for this decision is twofold. For one thing, if I am not alone with a guy, then I avoid even the possibility of stumbling. Secondly, the Bible says in 1 Thessalonians 5:22 that we are to avoid "all appearance of evil" (KJV). You may be alone with a guy and never do anything wrong, but there is no way for others to know what did or didn't go on. If there are others in the house, don't close the door to the room you are in. As believers, we should live above reproach. You never know who is watching and looking to you as their example. Let's not let our liberties cause others to stumble.

How Close Is Too Close?

I have often discussed with those in a relationship the question of "How close is too close?" I once heard a great analogy that helped answer that question. What do you tell a child who is near a dangerous cliff asking, "How close can I get without falling off?" The better question, as a parent knows, is "How far can we keep them away?" As you get to know someone and spend more time with him, it's natural that you want to be closer, but we need not to be naive about the temptations that can follow.

God created us as physical creatures, and there is a physical response in our bodies when attracted to someone of the opposite sex, especially when you begin to touch. I feel this issue is a prayerful matter and can be different for each couple. Here are a couple things that I believe are wise guidelines to follow though. Touching needs to be limited when it takes your mind to places you are not supposed to go yet—being blunt, I mean thinking about sleeping with the other person. Jesus says in Matthew 5:28 that if you even look at someone with lust, you have already committed adultery in your heart.

I also believe you need to take a step back if you are thinking more about what you can get from that person rather than thinking about simply being with the man himself. Are you excited to spend time talking with him and getting to know him better, or are you more focused on the way he makes you feel when you are with him? A relationship that is all about yourself is doomed to have problems.

So how close is too close when you are dating? My answer to this is another question, how much of yourself do you want to give to someone who is not your husband? You are a gift. Wouldn't it be nice to let your husband be the one to "unwrap" you?

We Need Each Other

Everyone has probably heard the scripture about the "fervent prayer of a righteous man avails much." But many times people forget or leave out the beginning of this verse, "Confess your trespasses to one another, and pray for one another, that you may be healed. The effective, fervent prayer of a righteous man avails much" James 5:16 (NKJV). Confess to one another. Pray for one another. We need one another! We need others to pray for us and surround our decisions and relationships in prayer.

I would encourage each of you to find an accountability partner. It is so important to have someone to share your dreams and hopes with as well as your downfalls and weaknesses. This person gives you accountability for the things you do or don't want to do in a relationship. An accountability partner also allows you to be strengthened and encouraged in the Lord and enables God's Word and truth to be spoken into your life. This is a person who loves you but is not afraid to tell you like it is. It should not be the person you are dating or are thinking about dating. It should be a woman that you feel comfortable talking to and can accept some constructive criticism from. We all need a voice of reason in our lives. When we are caught up in the romance and hope of the future, it is good to have someone with a voice of reason to keep your feet on the ground and at least help you look before you leap.

It is also a blessing to have an accountability partner, a friend, to go to when things don't work out and even when we fail to keep our boundaries. Ecclesiastes 4:10 says, "If one person falls, the other can reach out and help. But someone who falls alone is in real trouble" (NLT).

Protection Not Rejection

Something I prayed—with a sincere heart—was that I would have eyes for only my husband, that my husband would have eyes only for me, and that all others would be deflected. With that prayer, or should I say with the answer to that prayer, comes potential feelings of rejection. There have been plenty of guys around me I would have dated or would have at least liked to have been noticed by. I felt like I showed myself available, open, and friendly in conversations but to no avail. Most guys just weren't interested or were completely oblivious. Perhaps I just don't know how to flirt, ha! Oh well! I set it in my heart that the kind of man I feel God has for me will be the pursuer in our relationship, not the other way around. As I brought up earlier, Proverbs 18:22 says, "He who finds a wife finds a good thing, and obtains favor from the Lord" (NKJV). I believe that means the man is responsible for finding and pursuing the wife, not the other way around. I also believe if a relationship starts with the man taking the lead it will be easier to keep that order when you are married. It is God's design that a husband be head of the household and for women to come alongside.

As God answered my prayer, for eyes that weren't my husband's to be deflected, I found myself feeling a bit jealous of other ladies who were dating and getting engaged. I was fighting the feeling of rejection, wondering why no one was asking me out on a date. I believe this is not rejection by men but protection from God. When you are constantly being pursued, it brings a greater challenge of temptation and even confusion if you're unsure who you should be with. Perhaps there is someone who hangs on your every word, telling you things like you're beautiful, you're a treasure, or dare say it, "I love you." If this isn't the right guy, it would be hard to see and even harder to let go. Who wants to break up with a guy who makes you feel so special? Consider the possibility not being constantly pursued by men is actually a blessing in disguise. We are being protected by God, not rejected by men.

What If I Miss It?

A long-time struggle that I have dealt with is a fear that I would miss out on something important. When I was young, I had a huge dilemma any time I was faced with a decision that had more than one option. "Do I go with friends or spend time with Mom?" "Do I eat pizza or spaghetti?" "Do I… or do I…?" The problem was that I simply didn't want to miss out on anything. It seems as an adult, I carried some of that fear with me. What if I make a mistake? What if I don't choose the best option?

What if I miss out on what God wants for my life? That's a big deal! In Isaiah 30:21, God says, "Whether you turn to the right or to the left, your ears will hear a voice behind you, saying, 'This is the way; walk in it'" (NIV). No matter which way you go, God is there and will lead you. If the most important thing in your life is to love God and accomplish His will, He won't let you miss it. Honestly though, even if we did miss it, we probably wouldn't know it. And even if we knowingly make a mistake, I trust that our God is big enough to steer us back on track the moment we ask Him to.

In July 2013, I was at a Hillsong Conference in Sydney, Australia. My mom and I walked a little ways before the conference began to get a Starbucks—yes, even in Australia, thank You Jesus! While we were in line, we met two gentlemen from America. They had actually won the tickets to the conference. They were very nice guys… and really hot guys. On our way back to the conference, my mom said the taller one liked me (as moms do) and we should have exchanged e-mails. I said she was reading into it, but if God wanted us to meet again, then He could make that happen. All the while I'm thinking, "There's no way we'll run into them again. There are over twenty thousand people at this conference!" A few hours later, we got to the top of the Alphones Arena for one of the sessions and were sitting literally right next to them! It turned out he lived in the same city as one of my friends so we got all the information we needed, HA!

That man did not end up being my prince charming, but God did speak to me through this. He told me that no matter where I am, He sees me. He knows me. And He is God. If He wants me to meet someone, there is nothing that could stand in His way. He can cause someone to win a contest and get sent to the other side of the planet just to meet me if He wanted to—and He would do the same for you.

STUDY GUIDE

EN GARDE!

Key Points:

- "Guard your heart above all else, for it determines the course of your life" Proverbs 4:23 (NLT).

- Be mindful of the way you dress and the reasons for choosing your outfits. Are you dressing to draw the attention of men? Don't be the reason men stumble.

- It is essential to communicate your boundaries early on in a dating relationship. If he doesn't respect your boundaries from the start, then he is not the guy for you. Find out early and move on!

- Don't be discouraged if you haven't been asked out on a date in a while. Believe that God is looking out for you. You are being protected by God, not rejected by men.

- You are not going to miss it! Seek God's heart and will for your life first and foremost and He will lead you into all He desires for you.

Personal Reflection:

1. What are some ways you can guard your heart in relationships and still be open to love and sharing your life with someone?

_____

_____

_____

_____

_____

2. Have you ever been through a break up that left you feeling broken? How do you move past that feeling and leave with only a flesh wound?

_____

_____

_____

_____

_____

3. Who is your "accountability partner?" If you do not have one, think about who this woman could be and ask if she is willing to be someone you may talk to about difficult issues.

Accountability Partner:_____

"Confess your trespasses to one another, and pray for one another, that you may be healed. The effective, fervent prayer of a righteous man avails much."
James 5:16 (NKJV)

My Challenge to You:

I want you to think about your relationships with men, dating or otherwise. Write down some boundaries that you don't want to cross. Knowing ahead of time will help you avoid some awkward and potentially hazardous situations.

Time Alone:_____

_____

Touching:_____

_____

Hugs:_____

_____

Kisses:_____

_____

Sex:_____

_____

"I Love You":_____

_____

Other Boundaries:

_____

_____

_____

_____

Fun Extras!

Boundaries, book by Dr. Henry Cloud and Dr. John Townsend
Survival Guide for Young Women, book by
Holly Wagner and Nicole Reyes

CHAPTER 7

STANDING PURE

Do you know how lovely you are? If your first reaction to that question was to think something negative about yourself then you don't truly know who you are. You are BEAUTIFUL! God created you, and everything He creates is magnificent. He uniquely crafted every part of who you are from the color of your hair and eyes to your charming personality.

When you look in the mirror, do not criticize what you see but celebrate the beauty. Maybe you don't think you are beautiful, but whose eyes are you looking through, those of the world? If you step back and think about it, the world's idea of beauty is constantly changing and is only skin deep. There are so-called supermodels that in the world's eyes are gorgeous, but even many of them do not feel beautiful. Today most of us want to be thin and like to have a little suntan, but centuries ago, it was more attractive to be pale and a bit heavy set because that meant you had wealth, having enough money to eat well, and you didn't have to work all day in the sun.

Expectant mothers are said to be glowing because they are so excited they radiate joy and beauty. Those who know the Lord can be filled with joy that radiates love and true beauty. We need to be confident in the way God made us and know that we are beautiful to Him and that true beauty resonates from within. Proverbs 31:30 says, "Charm is deceptive, and beauty is fleeting; but a woman who fears the Lord is to be praised" (NIV). First Peter 3:3–4 puts it like this, "Your beauty should not come from outward adornment, such as elaborate hairstyles and the wearing of gold jewelry or fine clothes. Rather, it should be that of your inner self, the unfading beauty of a gentle and quiet spirit, which is of great worth in God's sight" (NIV). The New King James Version says, "Let it be the hidden person of the heart." It may sound cliché, but it's true, what matters most is what's on the inside.

God Didn't Mess Up

Another thought that struck me hard is that when I talk negatively about myself, I am actually telling God that what He created isn't good enough. I'm reminded of the scripture in Isaiah 45:9 that says, "What sorrow awaits those who argue with their Creator. Does a clay pot argue with its maker? Does the clay dispute with the one who shapes it, saying, 'Stop, you're doing it wrong!' Does the pot exclaim, 'How clumsy can you be?'" (NLT). And again in Romans 9:20, it says, "But who are you, a human being, to talk back to God? Shall what is formed say to the one who formed it, 'Why did you make me like this?'" (NIV). Ouch.

How dare we tell the Lord God Almighty, Creator of heaven and earth, that He messed up when He made us. No, our God did not mess up. You are not a mistake, no matter what the circumstances around your birth may say. Only God can give life, and He made you. You are beautiful and God has chosen you to be His. Know it. Love it. Live in that truth!

Pure Before The Lord

Some may read the title of this chapter and think, "How could I ever stand pure before God? If you only knew the things that I have done, the things I have thought, the things that have been done to me." Friend, I don't need to know because God already knows. I have good news and bad news for you though. The bad news is that we can never be good enough to stand pure before the Lord—not you, not me, not any of us. The good news, God made a way so we don't have to be good enough.

The answer to every Sunday school question, JESUS! Everyone has sinned in their lifetime. It may be something we consider small, like a little white lie, or it may be as big as murder. Sin is anything we do that is against the will of God. No matter how big or small the sin may be, the end result is the same, separation from God. On Earth, we measure sins by who they affect and the consequences that follow, but God looks at the heart.

Romans 3:23–24 says, "All have sinned and fall short of the glory of God, and all are justified freely by his grace through the redemption that came by Christ Jesus" (NIV). I also like how the Message's translation puts it. "Since we've compiled this long and sorry record as sinners (both us and them) and proved that we are utterly incapable of living the glorious lives God wills for us, God did it for us. Out of sheer generosity He put us in right standing with Himself. A pure gift. He got us out of the mess we're in and restored us to where He always wanted us to be. And He did it by means of Jesus Christ" (The Message).

When we accept Jesus as our Savior, all we need to do is ask God for forgiveness which He is more than happy to give no matter how badly or how often we mess up. Isaiah 1:18 says, "Though your sins are like scarlet, they shall be as white as snow; though they are red as crimson, they shall be like wool" (NKJV). God's forgiveness can wash you white as snow, TODAY!

Psalm 103:12 states, "He has removed our sins as far from us as the east is from the west" (NLT). When we ask God to forgive us, the Word says He has removed our sins as far as the east is from the west, which in case you haven't thought about how far that is, it's as far as they can possibly get! If you head east around the world you will never hit west. You'd have to turn around to head west and then you'd never hit east. Think of it in terms of the universe. Scientists believe that the universe and the stars are ever expanding. That means east and west will go on infinitely in opposite directions!

Start fresh today. His mercies are new every morning! No matter what you have done, the Bible says, "God's loyal love couldn't have run out, His merciful love couldn't have dried up. They're created new every morning. How great Your faithfulness! I'm sticking with God (I say it over and over). He's all I've got left" Lamentations 3:2–24 (The Message). When you feel like you are lost and have nothing left, God is there with arms open. He will restore your soul. He will renew your hope. God is not mad at you. He absolutely adores you! His love for you is great and unchanging. Don't listen to the lies that say you're not good enough or that you have to get right before coming to Him. He is waiting for you. Today can be a new beginning. Just turn to Him.

Used And Abused

Maybe it's not what you have done, but what's been done to you that makes you feel impure. It's been said that approximately one in five women have experienced sexual abuse. You may be one of the many women who have suffered and been used in this way, but that does not mean you are unclean, unworthy, or unlovable. You did not deserve what happened to you, and it was not your fault. You are beautiful, and when you accepted Jesus as Lord and Savior into your life, you were cleansed by the blood of Jesus. He cleansed us from our sins and the sins committed against us.

God likes to use the people the world sees as weak, like the young shepherd boy who slew the giant. In 1 Corinthians 1:27, it says, "But God chose the foolish things of the world to shame the wise; God chose the weak things of the world to shame the strong" (NIV). He chooses the unlikely to do great things. He befriends those the world calls rejects. The Bible says Jesus is a "friend of sinners… tax collectors… prostitutes." What the world despises, God treasures. He uses what the world has discarded and abused to create something beautiful.

God looks at us and sees the best version of ourselves. He sees us through the finished work Jesus did on the cross to pay for our sins. He sees us as the women He envisioned from before the foundations of the earth. He created you and loves you for exactly who you are.

Why God?

When I was eighteen years old, my youngest brother, Zak, had surgery to remove a brain tumor. The doctors said it was gone, but it was cancerous and could possibly come back. My family and friends prayed and believed that God had completely healed him. Everything went pretty much back to normal, but two years later, he began to exhibit symptoms and before we knew it, he had passed away. I was in shock. Confused and angry with God, I asked how He could let something like this happen to us. Why?

"Why God?" It's a question so many of us ask when awful things happen. When I asked, He didn't give me the answer I was looking for, but He did give me an answer that I believe can help us all. God graciously spoke this to my heart, "Stop looking for answers and instead search for peace." You won't find all the answers in life, and even if you did, it wouldn't change the situation; however, God does say He will give you the peace that surpasses all understanding. That's what He did for me, and that is what He can do for you. Where was God when this horrible thing happened? He was right there with us, not just watching but weeping with us and lightening the burden in ways we will never know with His incomprehensible grace. We live in a sinful, fallen world and the truth is, bad stuff happens as a result. The great news is that we have a God that we can trust even when things don't go the way we hope or plan.

Marriage, A Thing Of The Past?

There may be some of you reading this that are wondering if marriage is an old-fashioned idea. It is perfectly normal for guys and gals to live together before marriage or not plan to get married at all, right? Unfortunately, that is what we are surrounded with in today's culture. We are inundated with the propaganda that sex outside of marriage is normal and even the better way through movies, TV sit-coms, advertisements, and a hundred other avenues. I can guarantee you though this is not the best way. This is not God's way.

The Bible tells us specifically that sex outside of marriage is not the way God intended it. Not because He wants to hurt or frustrate us, but to keep us from deeper wounds that follow a lifestyle of promiscuity. In 1 Corinthians 6, it says, "There's more to sex than mere skin on skin. Sex is as much spiritual mystery as physical fact. As written in Scripture, "The two become one" (The Message). The two become one. How many people do you want to become one with? And if you sleep with someone then move on, you are leaving a part of yourself with them and taking a part of them with you into every other relationship you have. The chapter in 1 Corinthians goes on to say, "We must not pursue the kind of sex that avoids commitment and intimacy, leaving us more lonely than ever." I feel like that just about sums it up. The kind of sex that avoids commitment and intimacy, in other words sex without marriage, leaves us alone and eventually broken inside.

Have you heard the term soul ties? The *Urban Dictionary* defines the term like this:

> A spiritual/emotional connection you have to someone after being intimate with them, usually engaging in sexual intercourse. To the point that when you want to be rid of them from your mind and your life, even when you are far away from them and out of their presence you still feel as if they are a part of you and a part of you is with them, causing you to feel un-whole, as if you've given up some of yourself, intangible, that cannot be easily possessed again.[4]

From what I've gathered from others, that sounds about right. When you sleep with someone, you become a part of each other and enter into a relationship that is unique (or should be unique) to any other.

I have heard some people use the excuse for sex that they wouldn't buy a car without taking a "test drive." That's stupid. If you've never driven a car before, then the first one you drive will be awesome. The more people you have sex with, the worse it will be when you do get married. How hard will it be not to compare your spouse to the others you have slept with? Imagine how your spouse will feel knowing you are comparing them to another. I would imagine they would feel rather insecure or inadequate. If you wait to have sex until you are married, you don't bring that baggage into your marriage.

Maybe you've been divorced and think that strictly dating is the way to go. Marriage is too complicated, messy, and hard. You're right—it is hard! Paul says in 1 Corinthians 7:7–9, "Sometimes I wish everyone were single like me—a simpler life in many ways! But celibacy is not for everyone any more than marriage is. God gives the gift of the single life to some, the gift of the married life to others. I do, though, tell the unmarried and widows that singleness might well be the best thing for them, as it has been for me. But if they can't manage their desires and emotions, they should by all means go ahead and get married. The difficulties of marriage are preferable by far to a sexually tortured life as a single" (The Message). The thing is, to live according to the Word of God, you've got a life refraining from sex or you have marriage. I think it's hilarious how the Message states that it's preferable to get married than live "sexually tortured" as a single. I think that refers to tortured by desire as well as tortured by a life outside of the will of God.

Sex Outside Of Marriage

Sex outside of marriage is wrong. It's not an opinion; it is the Word of God. Please hear my heart. God loves you. I love you and do not want to judge or condemn you who have had or are having sex outside of marriage. I truly want the best God has for you and this is not it. God intended sex to be something amazing between a husband and a wife. He gave it as a gift, but He knows that sex outside of marriage will lead to hurt and brokenness for your heart. There may be temporary pleasure, but it will lead to an ultimate feeling of emptiness. When there is no commitment of marriage, it's easier for people to come and go as they please from one relationship to another.

This creates a soul tie and opens you up for a huge loss if they leave. "The two become one flesh." To separate will cause much pain.

God can take that pain and fill it with His unfailing love if you let Him. He takes you as you are, no matter what your current lifestyle is. Don't wait to get "fixed" to come to Him or come back to Him. He wants you now. Take a step toward Him and He will meet you. If you're caught in a cycle you don't know how to get out of, He's the best man for the job. When you ask for God's forgiveness and take that step toward Him, you are made pure. When you accept Jesus' love and forgiveness into your life, God sees you through Him. Every day is a new day to decide how you're going to live. The string of yesterday's decisions are in the past, and you can choose to make a good decision today.

You can do it. You have everything you need to live a life that glorifies God. First Corinthians 1:7–9 says, "You don't need a thing, you've got it all! All God's gifts are right in front of you as you wait expectantly for our Master Jesus to arrive on the scene for the Finale. And not only that, but God himself is right alongside to keep you steady and on track until things are all wrapped up by Jesus. God, who got you started on this spiritual adventure, shares with us the life of His Son and our Master Jesus. He will never give up on you. Never forget that" (The Message). God never gives up on you!

Momentary Guilt Versus True Repentance

Do you remember being a kid and getting in trouble? Well, it never happened to me, but it happened to my brother all the time! ☺ There were times when I'll bet he was deeply and genuinely sorry for what he had done wrong, and he promised our parents that it would never happen again. Then there were times that he got caught in something he wasn't supposed to be doing, and he was sorry too. Sorry he got caught! He probably gritted his teeth and said "I'm sorry," but in his heart, he really wasn't.

There is a difference between saying I'm sorry and truly repenting. It is an issue of the heart followed by an action. It means you are sorry for the things that you've done wrong, and you take steps not to repeat mistakes in the future. You set your mind to going a different direction. The dictionary defines repent[5] as "to feel such sorrow for sin or fault as to be disposed to change one's life for the better." Repentance is changing your ways. It isn't knowingly continuing in sin and thinking it will be okay because you can keep asking for forgiveness later. In Romans 6:1–2, Paul mockingly says, "So what do we do? Keep on sinning so God can keep on forgiving? I should hope not!" (The Message).

Be careful if you are choosing to live in sin. It is a trap that you can get caught in today, which could ensnare not only your future, but also your soul. Hebrews 10:26–27 says, "For if we sin willfully after we have received the knowledge of the truth, there no longer remains a sacrifice for sins, but a certain fearful expectation of judgment, and fiery indignation which will devour the adversaries" (NKJV). I don't want any of you living in fear of eternity and neither does God. Make a decision today and ask God to help you out if you find yourself in a cycle of sin. It doesn't matter how long it has been. Take a first step toward Him right now by saying in your heart, "Help me, Jesus." He will give you the next step and help you along the way.

I'm Expecting!

I'm expecting! Now, what did you think when you read that phrase? No, I'm not pregnant, but I had you there for a second, right? I am expectant though. I am expecting good things to come my way. I'm expecting that the Lord will lead me in the way He wants me to go. I'm expecting that in God's perfect timing, He will maneuver myself and my future husband to finally meet, date, and get married. I'm expecting that someday I will be expecting because that is a desire of my heart. I have hope that someday these things will come to pass.

When someone is truly expecting, a baby that is, it is important that they prepare. We have nine months to prepare when we are pregnant, and I think the Lord was purposeful in giving us that time. It allows us to prepare the home for a new arrival. It gives us time to get things in order and buy everything that the new little one will need—bed, clothes, stroller, car seat, and a billion other things I'm sure. Having nine months also gives us time to mentally prepare for the changes to come although I've heard you can never be fully prepared.

Maybe thinking about expecting a baby is a little much for you. What do you do when you are expecting a guest at your house for dinner or if you are planning for an event with multiple guests? You need to straighten the house, sweep the floors, clean the bathroom, make the bed, etc. Don't forget to send an invitation. You also want to make sure you have something prepared for them to eat and probably have some plan in mind for the evening.

My point is that if you are expecting, you need to prepare. If you were planning an event but did nothing to prepare, the event probably wouldn't happen at all. If it did happen, it would be an utter catastrophe. I'm not saying to plan your wedding and send out invitations before you've met the groom but think about the things in your life that you can prepare now. Ask yourself, "Am I the person I desire to be when I get married? If not, how can I adjust things now?"

For myself, I want to be healthy, spiritually and physically fit! Am I doing anything to work on those goals now? Well, I occasionally work out but not on a regular basis. Am I reading the Bible and spending quiet time with God? Yes, but not as in depth or as often as I'd like to. How about you? Are there things you'd like to see different in your life? Let's make an effort and make a plan to change them. We can set a schedule for ourselves, put reminders in our phones, get accountability partners, and get our booties in motion!

Are you expecting? Or should I say, are you expectant? I want to challenge you to be expecting the things that you are hoping for in life. Be expectant and then prepare thusly.

I am expecting good things today, are you? You know, when I look for something, I usually find it. If I'm looking for the worst in a person or situation, I'm going to find it, but when I'm looking for the best, that's what I'll discover. If we start our day looking for the good, we are much more likely to find it. Let's look together, shall we?

"God, who got you started on this spiritual adventure, shares with us the life of His Son and our Master Jesus. He will never give up on you. Never forget that."
1 Corinthians 1:9 (The Message)

STUDY GUIDE

STANDING PURE

Key Points:

- You are BEAUTIFUL! You are a treasure, chosen, and unique.

- Start fresh today. His mercies are new every morning! No matter what you have done, "God's loyal love couldn't have run out, His merciful love couldn't have dried up. They're created new every morning" Lamentations 3:22–23 (The Message).

- When you feel like you are lost and have nothing left, God is there with arms open. He will restore your soul. He will renew your hope. His love for you is great and unchanging. Today can be a new beginning. Just turn to Him.

- Sometimes we have to stop looking for answers and instead search for peace because even if we had the answers, it wouldn't change the circumstance. God can give us the grace and peace for every situation.

- Expect good things to happen today! Look for them and I bet you will find them.

Personal Reflection:

1. How do you see yourself?

_____

_____

_____

_____

_____

2. Was the previous answer mostly positive or negative? Add three positive traits.

_____

_____

_____

_____

_____

3. Have you ever asked, "Why God?" If so, what was the answer?

_____

_____

_____

_____

_____

4. Is there anything in your life that you need to repent of? How can you take the first step down a different path?

_____

_____

_____

_____

_____

5. What are you expectant of in the next year and what can you do to prepare?

_____

_____

_____

_____

_____

Fun Extras!
"How Can It Be," song by Lauren Daigle
"Strong Enough," song by Stacie Orrico
"This Love Song," song by Amanda Wilders
"Just Be Held," song by Casting Crowns
"I Believe," song by Wilders Worship
Captivating, book by John and Stasi Eldredge

"Your beauty should not come from outward adornment, such as elaborate hairstyles and the wearing of gold jewelry or fine clothes. Rather, it should be that of your inner self, the unfading beauty of a gentle and quiet spirit, which is of great worth in God's sight."

1 Peter 3:3–4 (NIV)

---- **CHAPTER 8** ----

WHO'S YOUR DADDY?

You are the daughter of the King of Kings, which makes you a princess in the most glorious kingdom ever known to man. AWESOME, RIGHT!?! When we make a decision to follow Jesus, God brings us into His family. Ephesians 1:5 says, "God decided in advance to adopt us into his own family by bringing us to himself through Jesus Christ. This is what he wanted to do, and it gave him great pleasure" (NLT). The Word also tells us in Romans 8:16–17 that "The Spirit himself testifies with our spirit that we are God's children. Now if we are children, then we are heirs—heirs of God and co-heirs with Christ" (NIV). We are children of the King and have a great inheritance in store.

Father God

"Our Father in heaven, hallowed be Your name" (NIV). When asked by His disciples how to pray, Jesus responded with these words in Matthew 6. That was a new concept and hard for those in that time to accept. Many of the Pharisees even sought Jesus' life because of this teaching. The Bible in John 5:18 says, "Therefore the Jews sought all the more to kill Him, because He not only broke the Sabbath, but also said that God was His Father, making Himself equal with God" (NKJV).

People still have a difficult time grasping this concept of God as "Father," and I believe a great factor in how we view God is the relationship we have with our earthly father. In today's culture, fathers have become less and less active in the lives of their children, their positions in the home have weakened, and the respect that was once inherently given is now a rarity to find.

We see several types of fathers in the world around us. There are just a few broad examples that I want to look at more closely. We have the cruel, abusive father. This man is selfish and his harsh lifestyle takes a toll and brings much pain to his child. He does not show love or give affirmation. He is extreme in his discipline, often without cause.

Another example would be the conditional father. This is the type of father who loves his child but with "strings attached." This father shows love to the child but only when he/she "deserves" it. He disciplines too harshly, at times, for the unmet expectation. He wants to do right by his child, but his expectations leave his child continually striving and always falling short of the demands placed.

His child can be left with feelings of failure and a constant struggle with rejection.

The next example is the absent father. This father, sadly, is a growing category in our society. He is not involved or is "in and out" of his child's life. He is unreliable and unfaithful. He may be mysterious, never known by his child. His child may be left in bitterness and resentment toward the father or feel a hurt and disappointment toward the father. His child may feel like there's always something missing, an emptiness only filled when God has met that need.

The last example I'd like to consider is the loving, doting father. This is the man who loves his child unconditionally, to the best of his ability. He makes sacrifices for his child. He is balanced in love and discipline. He guides his child through life, teaching the child as he/she grows. He desires to give good gifts to his child and to see him/her prosper in all things.

Many times the view we have of our earthly father reflects the view we capture of our heavenly father. If our father was abusive, we expect judgment and punishment from God. If he was "conditional," we constantly strive for the approval of God by doing "good works." We also may feel that if we fail or don't do enough, God no longer loves and accepts us. If our father was absent or in and out of our lives, we may see God in that same manner—questioning His faithfulness or possibly just not understanding how to relate to God as "Father."

Who Is He To You?

My dad was by no means perfect, but he was more toward the loving, doting father. He loved me and my siblings like crazy; maybe a bit light on the discipline, but that's what he had mom for, right

LOL! I have always related to God in this way as well. I know He loves me and nothing I do could ever change that.

No earthly father is perfect, for "all have sinned, and fallen short of the glory of God." But we have a heavenly Father to look to though men fail us. As we try to imagine what a perfect father would look like, we catch a glimpse of who our God wants to be to us. God is the Loving, Doting Father. His love for us is unconditional. In the original Greek translation of the Bible, the word used for God's love toward us is agape. Agape is an unconditional, unmerited, and self-less love. He would sacrifice everything for us. John 3:16 says, "For God so loved the world, that He gave His only begotten Son, that whoever believes in Him should not perish, but have everlasting life" (NKJV). He gave His most precious possession for us.

He also loves us enough to discipline us. Proverbs 3:10–11 states, "Do not despise the chastening of the Lord, nor detest His correction; for whom the Lord loves He corrects, just as a father the son in whom he delights" (NKJV). God leads His children and guides our steps. Proverbs 3:5–6 says, "Trust in the Lord with all your heart, and lean not on your own understanding; in all your ways acknowledge Him, and He shall direct your paths" (NKJV). His desire is for us and He loves to give good gifts to His children. Matthew 7:9–11 says, "What man is there among you who, if his son asks for bread, will give him a stone? Or if he asks for a fish, will he give him a serpent? If you then, being evil, know how to give good gifts to your children, how much more will your Father who is in heaven give good things to those who ask Him!" (NKJV).

We need to know God, not only as Lord and Savior, but as a loving Father. We are "adopted" as children of God and share in the full inheritance of Christ. We are children of God. Galatians 4:6–7 says, "You can tell for sure that you are now fully adopted as his own children because God sent the Spirit of his Son into our lives crying out, 'Papa! Father!' Doesn't that privilege of intimate conversation with God make it plain that you are not a slave, but a child? And if you are a child, you're also an heir, with complete access to the inheritance" (The Message).

I love this verse from the Message version of the Bible. Romans 8:15–17 says, "This resurrection life you received from God is not a timid, grave-tending life. It's adventurously expectant, greeting God with a childlike 'What's next, Papa?' God's Spirit touches our spirits and confirms who we really are. We know who He is, and we know who we are: Father and children. And we know we are going to get what's coming to us—an unbelievable inheritance! We go through exactly what Christ goes through. If we go through the hard times with Him, then we're certainly going to go through the good times with Him!" Knowing who God is and how He sees us begins to reveal who we are. We should pray that God would reveal Himself to us as Father in a greater way and turn our hearts to Him.

How do you see God? Father? Friend? Comforter? Dictator? Far away and unreachable? Uncaring and indifferent? How you see God can reflect on how you see yourself. Your value does not come from what you do or your relationship status. It comes from knowing who you are because of Whose you are.

Do you love yourself? That may seem like an odd question, and many of us would say no. For one thing, that would seem narcissistic. Also, most of us if we're honest would like to change a thing or two about ourselves. Well, I'm here to tell you that God NEEDS you to love yourself. Matthew 22:39 is one of the greatest commandments Jesus gave us. It says to "love your neighbor as yourself" (NKJV). How can you love your neighbor if you don't even like yourself? Know that God created you to be just who you are and He doesn't make any mistakes. As we embrace this and learn to love ourselves, we are able to love others and be a light to those who don't yet know Him.

When you look in the mirror, do you see how great you look or is the first thing you notice something negative? As women, we usually are the most critical of ourselves. We see our faults and blemishes and want to fix or hide them. I have been guilty of this myself, but I'm here to tell you that God sees you as beautiful, perfectly made by the Perfect Creator.

"It's adventurously expectant, greeting God with a child-like "What's next, Papa?" We know who He is, and we know who we are: Father and children."

Romans 8:15–17 (The Message)

What Is Love?

My last boyfriend told me he loved me less than two months after we started seeing each other. I didn't give him quite the response he was looking for. I told him that I thought I loved him, but that I really wasn't sure what this kind of love was. I love my family, I love my friends, I love cheese pizza, but I felt like there was a different weight to the word love when I consider saying it to a man, and there is. The relationship between man and woman, and one day husband and wife, is unique to any other relationship. It comes with its own responsibilities, holds a level of trust and commitment, and there is an understanding of promises between the two.

During this time, I prayed and asked the Lord to help me understand love in a new way. I heard a great song on the radio called

"More Like Falling in Love" by Jason Gray. I asked the Lord, "How do I fall in love?" and "How do I know if I'm in love?" He sweetly whispered to my heart, "How did you fall in love with Me?"

I love God with all my heart, but I love Him because He found me and first loved me. I fell in love with Him by learning more about Him through the Bible, spending time with Him, and simply talking with Him. The better I get to know God, the more I love Him. God said that's the same way we'll fall in love. There will be a man blessed enough to find you, and he will pursue your heart. He will fall for you, and you will be drawn to him.

How did we fall in love with Jesus? I think we met Him and something about Jesus attracted us to Him. We were drawn to Him. Then we chose to be in relationship with Him; we chose to love Him. The more time we spent with Him, the better we got to know Him, and the more we trusted Him. As we got to know Him better, we grew in our relationship with Him. We loved Him more and more. I venture to say that falling in love with a man is very similar. We meet and something about him draws us to him. We spend time with him and get to know him better. We develop trust and grow in relationship with each other. Then we choose to love him.

Love Is A Choice

Isn't it sweet how some couples have "their song?" It symbolizes their love for each other and perhaps reminds them of a special moment they shared. I too have a song for that "special" moment shared, a break-up song! When my boyfriend decided to break up with me, there was a song playing in the background called "Chasing Cars" by Snow Patrol. Part of the song says, "Those three words are said too much. They're not enough." Amen! As I was being dumped, my boyfriend said a few things that didn't quite sit well with me. Set aside the fact that he was dumping me, but how he did it and what he said really caught me off guard. He told me that he didn't love me anymore. I was a bit dumbfounded (because I'm such an amazing person ☺), but I tried to understand how he could so quickly change his mind while I was on vacation. I had been gone a whole 9 days, so clearly that was enough time to fall out of love! I asked him what love was to him, and he replied, "It's just how I *felt* in the moment." Shortly after that, we parted and haven't spoken much since. It did get me thinking about love though. You see, I believe love is first and foremost a choice that we make, not an emotion we feel. Also, a side note for any guys reading this, you don't take a girl to a public restaurant to break up with her. None of us want to bawl our eyes out in front of a bunch of strangers!

It is important to keep your heart and emotions in check when you are in a relationship. Yes, emotions play a part in knowing the person God has for you, but they should be tempered by wisdom and self-control. If you are not careful, you can "fall in love" with the wrong guy simply because your emotions got the best of you. Trust me, you may feel like you are in love, but your feelings can deceive you. You can choose to love someone, and you can choose how to deal with your feelings. Your emotions are a part of who you are, but they should not be allowed to control you. "Learn to love appropriately. You need to use your head and test your feelings so that your love is sincere and intelligent, not sentimental gush" Philippians 1:9–10 (The Message).

Love is also an action. In 1 John 3:18, it says, "Dear children, let us not love with words or speech but with actions and in truth" (NIV). Most of us have also heard the "love" chapter in 1 Corinthians 13. It says, "Love is patient, love is kind. It does not envy, it does not boast, it is not proud. It does not dishonor others, it is not self-seeking, it is not easily angered, it keeps no record of wrongs. Love does not delight in evil but rejoices with the truth. It always protects, always trusts, always hopes, always perseveres. Love never fails" (NIV). These aren't just sweet words; they are words to live by. Just saying we love someone doesn't make it true. It is evidenced by how it is outworked in our lives, by the fruit around us. Do I walk in love? We must ask ourselves, "Am I patient and self-sacrificing to those around me? Do I tell the truth when it's easier to lie? Do I forgive or do I hold a grudge?"

Read it in the Message translation, slowly, line by line:

"Love never gives up.
Love cares more for others than for self. Love doesn't want what it doesn't have. Love doesn't strut,
Doesn't have a swelled head, Doesn't force itself on others, Isn't always "me first," Doesn't fly off the handle,
Doesn't keep score of the sins of others, Doesn't revel when others grovel,
Takes pleasure in the flowering of truth, Puts up with anything,
Trusts God always, Always looks for the best,
Never looks back, but keeps going to the end."
1 Corinthians 13:4–7 (The Message)

Does any of that look like an emotional response? Do we really ever feel like doing all these things or do we have to make the choice? We choose to put others before ourselves. We choose to look for the best in people, and we choose, umm, well no, we try really, really hard not to "fly off the handle" when people tick us off, right?

These are aspects of true love. You may think you love someone, but if you don't respect them, if you're not patient and kind toward them, then it is not genuine love. It is a fleeting feeling and people's reasoning behind falling "out of love." To fall out of love is not a true thing it all. It's really just a thing that leaves room for the excuse of jumping from one relationship to the next.

Peace For Today, Trust For Tomorrow

As I was dating, the Lord revealed many pearls of wisdom that I am so grateful for. One day I was walking along the beautiful beaches of Destin asking the Lord if being with this man was God's plan for my life. I just wanted the Lord to say, "Yes, marry him" or "No, keep waiting." What I got instead was the sense of Father God smiling at me and saying, "I will give you the answers you need when you need them. I will give you peace and grace for today. Enjoy today and trust in Me for tomorrow."

"A man's heart plans his way, but the Lord directs his steps" Proverbs 16:9 (NKJV). My plans have changed so many times over the last year, but I know the Lord has directed them. I was completely undone at one point in my life when I received a prophetic word that went something like this: "You have your plans about the future, and they are all written out, but the Lord says they are written in chalk, and He is about to wipe it all away. It won't be left blank though." How is that for an encouraging word? I wasn't very excited to hear it, but I learned to trust the Lord even more. My plan was to get married and start a family. I even had the most beautiful ring picked out! Turned out, that wasn't God's plan. I did not marry the man I was dating, obviously, and I actually ended up in Australia! That is another story for another time though. Through everything I held on to these words, "Peace for today. Trust for tomorrow." I needed that reminder from God to keep me going. He offers those words to you as well. He will give you all that you need for today and comfort you with His peace in every decision as you trust Him.

This year the Lord has been teaching me to walk in faith as I never have before. With that I can see Him preparing me to be the woman He desires me to be, and someday the wife my future husband will need. Allow Him to work in you as well, sweet daughter of the King.

Who I Am In Christ

Below are statements of truth along with scriptures about who you are in Christ. Don't skim through them but read all of them at least once, aloud if you are in a place where you are able to. These are great confessions that you need to know and believe. I also encourage you to pick a few favorites and put them on sticky notes around your house and in your car.

~ I Am Loved by God
   John 17:23 "The world will know that you sent me and have loved them even as you have loved me" (NIV).

~ I Am Fearfully and Wonderfully Made
   Psalm 139:14 "I praise you because I am fearfully and wonderfully made; your works are wonderful, I know that full well" (NIV).

~ I Am God's Workmanship
   Ephesians 2:10 "For we are His workmanship, created in Christ Jesus for good works, which God prepared beforehand that we should walk in them" (NKJV).

~ I Am the Light of the World
   Matthew 5:14 "You are the light of the world—like a city on a hilltop that cannot be hidden" (NLT).

~ I Am the Apple of My Father's Eye
   Psalm 17:8 "Keep me as the apple of your eye; hide me in the shadow of your wings" (NIV).

~ I Am a Child of God
   John 1:12 "But to all who believed him and accepted him, he gave the right to become children of God" (NLT).

~ I Am a Friend of Jesus
John 15:15 "I no longer call you servants, because a servant does not know his master's business. Instead, I have called you friends, for everything that I learned from my Father I have made known to you" (NIV).

~ I Am the Righteousness of God in Christ
2 Corinthians 5:21 "For He made Him who knew no sin to be sin for us, that we might become the righteousness of God in Him" (NKJV).

~ I Am Free from Condemnation
Romans 8:1 "So now there is no condemnation for those who belong to Christ Jesus" (NLT).

~ I Am Dead to Sin and Alive to God
Romans 6:11 "So you also should consider yourselves to be dead to the power of sin and alive to God through Christ Jesus" (NLT).

~ I Am Redeemed and Forgiven
Ephesians 1:7 "He is so rich in kindness and grace that he purchased our freedom with the blood of his Son and forgave our sins" (NLT).

~ I Am Complete in Him
Colossians 2:10 "And you are complete in Him, who is the head of all principality and power" (NKJV).

~ I Am Accepted in Him
Romans 15:7 "Accept one another, then, just as Christ accepted you, in order to bring praise to God" (NIV).

~ I Am Free from Sickness and Disease
Matthew 8:17 "He took our sicknesses and removed our diseases" (NLT).

~ I Am Healed and Made Whole
1 Peter 2:24 "He himself bore our sins in his body on the cross, so that we might die to sins and live for righteousness; 'by his wounds you have been healed" (NIV).

~ I Am Filled with Peace
Philippians 4:7 "And the peace of God, which surpasses all understanding, will guard your hearts and minds through Christ Jesus" (NKJV).

~ I Am Provided For
Philippians 4:19 "And my God shall supply all your need according to His riches in glory by Christ Jesus" (NKJV).

~ I Am More Than a Conqueror
Romans 8:37 "Yet in all these things we are more than conquerors through Him who loved us" (NKJV).

~ I Am Bold and Confident
Ephesians 3:12 "Because of Christ and our faith in him, we can now come boldly and confidently into God's presence" (NLT).

~ I Am a New Creation in Christ
1 Corinthians 5:17 "Therefore, if anyone is in Christ, he is a new creation; old things have passed away; behold, all things have become new" (NKJV).

~ I Am Sealed with the Holy Spirit of Promise
Ephesians 1:13 "In Him you also trusted, after you heard the word of truth, the gospel of your salvation; in whom also, having believed, you were sealed with the Holy Spirit of promise" (NKJV).

~ I Am Holy and Pure Before God
  Ephesians 1:4 "Even before he made the world, God loved us and chose us in Christ to be holy and without fault in his eyes" (NLT).

~ I Am Blessed with Every Spiritual Blessing
  Ephesians 1:3 "All praise to God, the Father of our Lord Jesus Christ, who has blessed us with every spiritual blessing in the heavenly realms because we are united with Christ" (NLT).

~ I Am Chosen
  1 Thessalonians 1:4 "We know, dear brothers and sisters, that God loves you and has chosen you to be his own people" (NLT).

STUDY GUIDE

WHO'S YOUR DADDY?

Key Points:

- When we know who God is, we know who we truly are.

- God is the Loving, Doting Father. His love for us is unconditional.

- You are the daughter of the King of Kings, which makes you a princess in the most glorious kingdom ever known to man.

- Love is more than an emotion we feel, but a choice we make that is evidenced by our actions. You can choose to love someone, and you can choose how to deal with your feelings.

"You can tell for sure that you are now fully adopted as His own children because God sent the Spirit of His Son into our lives crying out, "Papa! Father!"

Doesn't that privilege of intimate conversation with God make it plain that you are not a slave, but a child? And if you are a child, you're also an heir, with complete access to the inheritance."
Galatians 4:6–7 (The Message)

Personal Reflection:

1. What type of earthly father did you have?

   _____

   _____

   _____

   _____

   _____

2. If your natural father was absent in your life, is there a spiritual "father figure" you could look up to?

   _____

   _____

   _____

   _____

   _____

3. How has your earthly father affected your view of your heavenly Father?

   _____

   _____

   _____

   _____

   _____

4. What are the first three words/phrases that come to mind when you hear the word God?

   _____

   _____

   _____

   _____

   _____

5. How do the words you just wrote relate to you?

_____

_____

_____

_____

_____

6. How does God see you?

_____

_____

_____

_____

_____

7. Was your answer from question six positive or negative?

If negative, then your view of your Father God needs to be shifted. Recognize the need to change your perspective and continue to build relationship with the Father God who loves you. A good start is to review the "I Am…" statements in chapter 8. Pick three that talk about how God sees you and write them down. Put them in a place that you will see them throughout the day and be reminded of His great love for you.

8. Read 1 Corinthians 13 replacing the word "love" with your name. How do you measure up?

_____

_____

_____

_____

_____

My Challenge to You:

Find an index card or piece of paper and write the below phrases down. Put them on your mirror and say them each once a day while looking at yourself. They are so true, and eventually, I know you will believe them.

~ God Loves Me ~

~ I Love Myself ~

~ I Am Beautiful ~

Take some time and ask God how He sees you. Write down a few words about how He uniquely sees you. If you are having trouble, look back to the section in chapter 8 called "Who I Am in Christ." Read each "I Am…" confession and choose the one that, in your heart, you have trouble truly believing:

_____
_____
_____
_____
_____

Fun Extras!
"How He Loves Us," song by Kim Walker
"More Like Falling in Love," song by Jason Gray
"Mystery," song by Gateway Worship
"Show Me Your Face," song by Wilders Worship
"Single and Not Waiting," article by Rachel Selinger

CHAPTER 9

SHALL WE DANCE?

God's Invitation

I want to take you back to the beginning of the book as I shared with you about this dance of life. The Lord gave me such a clear picture of what married life could be like depending on the man I choose. A word from the Lord was all I needed to hear, so I shared my heart with my boyfriend back then and, as nicely as I could, broke it off. Not an easy thing to do, but I felt such peace because I knew that God had spoken to me. God assured me that He had somebody in mind, someone set apart for me.

At that time, I told the Lord that I was content to just "sit out of the dance" until He brought me the right person. This is what I want you to get though. God sweetly told me, "I don't want you to sit out of the dance. While you wait, I am your dance partner. I am holding you close, and My Holy Spirit will lead you with a gentle nudge to your back or whisper in your ear. Then, in the right timing, I will graciously let your husband cut-in."

How great is our God!?! I believe this is true for each of us, my friend. He is truly the ultimate gentleman! God doesn't want you sitting out of the dance of life, and He doesn't want you feeling desperate or alone. He wants you to know Him intimately. He wants to whisper in your ear how beautiful you are and how much He loves you. When we know that, we will be not only content but excited to dance with our God. When our husband comes along, he will seamlessly and naturally cut-in.

Trust God. He cares even more about your future than you do. God is reaching His hand out to you asking, "Shall We Dance?" Will you accept His invitation? He is a loving God who only wants the best for you. He desires your heart and your devotion. What will your response be?

I am not sure where you are on this journey of life, but I need to ask, do you know this God that I know? Have you had an encounter with Jesus? He is my best friend, my confidante, the love of my life, and the reason for rising every morning.

Who is He to you? Does He seem near to you or far? A friend you can share your deepest feelings and fears with or an angry God you rarely speak to? My friend, God wants to be your everything. He had you in mind when He formed this world, and He has you in mind today. He sent His most precious possession, His Son Jesus, to die so He could be in relationship with you. Do you know this God I know? If you do, then I tell you He wants to be even closer than ever before, for there is so much more of Him to know!

If you do not know Him, if you have walked away from Him or if you just aren't quite sure, then I hope you will decide to wait no longer. He has been pursuing you and all you have to do is turn to Him. I implore you to say this prayer and mean it with all of your heart:

> Father God, I know that I am a sinner in need of a Savior. I believe that you sent Your Son, Jesus, to die for me and that You raised Him from the dead so that I could be saved. I want you to be Lord and Savior of my life. Help me to live for You and be satisfied in You alone. In Jesus' name, amen.

It's that simple. Romans 10:9 says, "If you declare with your mouth, 'Jesus is Lord,' and believe in your heart that God raised Him from the dead, you will be saved" (NIV). The angels are rejoicing as you have stepped into the Kingdom of God, and I celebrate with you too!

Our Plans Vs. God's Plans

I have discovered in recent years that many times our plan and God's plan can look a little different. For instance, I told God years ago that I thought twenty-four would be the perfect age to get married. Then we could wait about a year and a half to have our first child, a blonde-haired, blue-eyed little girl who would be just like her momma. Then we would wait another year and have a little boy. I even picked out names! Well, God had other plans, and when twenty-four came and went, I had a choice to make. I could either give my plans to God and trust that He had better ones, or I could take matters into my own hands and settle for less than His best. I chose to trust God.

"I know the plans I have for you,' says the Lord."
Jeremiah 29:11 (NLT)

It has taken me years, but I have finally gotten to a place where I can say this honestly, "If God never did another thing for me, He has already done enough. If "Mr. Right" never comes along, God is enough." I challenge you to check your heart and ask yourself if God is enough for you. If you never get married, will you and God still be on good speaking terms? Be honest with yourself. It is okay to say no, but you do need to understand that it is an area that you need to let go of and come to terms with. He gave His most precious possession, His only Son, Jesus Christ, to die for us. Jesus took our sins upon Himself, died, and rose again so we could be saved. We have a place in heaven with God for eternity because of what He did for us. If our God never does anything else, salvation is more than enough. Relationship with Him is more than enough.

There are some people who will never get married. We have all probably met someone who stayed single, and I believe there are some people God has called to remain that way. As Paul says in 1 Corinthians 7:7, "Sometimes I wish everyone were single like me—a simpler life in many ways! But celibacy is not for everyone any more than marriage is. God gives the gift of the single life to some, the gift of the married life to others" (The Message).

To be married is a gift, but singleness is a gift as well. The single woman does not have the time constraints that the married does and can be completely devoted to the things of God without the concerns that come with a husband and children. Never despise the season you are in or waste it away wishing for the next. As you are seeking God, the next season will come in His timing.

Psalm 37:4 says, "Delight yourself also in the Lord and He shall give you the desires of your heart" (NKJV). I believe God puts certain desires in your heart, and since you are reading this book, I think it's safe to say marriage is one of them. The best part is, God wants to grant you that desire! Take delight in the Lord. Trust in God with all your heart because He loves you and wants to bless you—His beloved daughter. God knew us in our mothers' wombs, He formed and fashioned every detail from the color of our eyes to our unique personalities. He is a loving God that is into the details of our lives. Don't you believe He has also thought about the future husband you will have? My greatest hope for you is that you will not settle for anything less than God's best.

Single And Loving It!

The single life is awesome! Well, it certainly can be. I know most of us singles will have our lonely days and at times, feel a longing for a husband and family. Those days don't have to be the focus of our lives though, and neither should they be. Enjoy the single life! For today we may be called to be single but with that comes a lot less responsibility as well as more free time. We can devote more time to God in prayer and studying His Word. We can go places and do things as a single that would be a lot harder with a family in tow, and a lot more expensive! Personally, I was able to spend a year in Australia studying worship and theology. I took a short missions trip to Rome. I took a vacation to travel through Europe starting in London then to Paris, Venice, and

Rome, followed by a cruise where I visited Florence, Pisa, Naples, Marseille, and Barcelona. Jealous much? Don't be, just do it! At least do something while you are single that maybe you won't be able to do if and when you get married. Cherish the season you are in because it won't last forever.

Usually when we hear the words, "I will do this when I get this," it is just an excuse not to start something now. Don't wait for a man to come along to start living your life. Maybe all you dreamed of when you were younger was to be married and raise a family, but perhaps God's plans are a little different. Maybe He has something for you to do now that you couldn't do if you were married. See what God has put in your hands today and make the most of it. Be a good steward of what He has given you to make a difference. I once heard someone say, "I can't do everything, but I MUST do something." You can do something today with what you have (your gifts, talents, money, time, etc.) and reach people for His glory. Ask God what He would have you do right now. I decided to write a book, ha!

What is God trying to teach you right now? Is there something He wants you to learn in this season so the next season won't be as difficult? Maybe He has more for you to learn before you get married so that your future marriage will flourish, for example, you may need to learn to manage an anger problem or to develop patience. God is preparing you today for who He has called you to be tomorrow. As one of my trainers said in Bible College, "Preparation time is never wasted time." God can use every event that has happened in your life to make you a better person—to make you more like Him.

Your Love Story

God has a plan and a love story in mind for you! It will be uniquely yours, and trust me it will be worth the wait! The longer the wait, the sweeter the appreciation. I am still single and waiting with you, but I have hope that in God's perfect timing Mr. Right will come along for each of us. I am confident that God's plans are greater than ours, and He will lead us on the right path for our lives. Continue to pursue Jesus and trust Him with your heart. Remember that your love story doesn't start when you meet Prince Charming. It starts now.

Thank you for journeying with me through this season of my life. I am so excited that I could share it with you! I hope and pray that the Lord has used this to minister to you in some way. God has great things in store for your life and will lead you one day at a time.

I don't want you to sit out of the dance. While you wait...
I Am your dance partner.
I Am holding you close.
My Holy Spirit will lead you.

STUDY GUIDE

SHALL WE DANCE?

Key Points:

- Our plans are not always God's plans.

- If God never did another thing for us, He has already done enough. If "Mr. Right" never comes along, God is enough.

- The single life is awesome! ENJOY IT!

- Preparation time is never wasted time. God has a plan and a love story in mind for you. It will be uniquely yours, and trust me it will be worth the wait! The longer the wait, the sweeter the appreciation.

- Your love story doesn't start when you meet Prince Charming. It starts now.

Personal Reflection:

1. Would you be okay if you never get married? Will you and God be on good terms if He did not have that in mind for your future? Be honest.

   _____

   _____

   _____

   _____

   _____

2. Is there anything that you have wanted to do in life but have been putting off? What is it and how can you take a step toward that goal?

_____

_____

_____

_____

_____

3. If you could do one thing before you get married, what would it be?

_____

_____

_____

_____

_____

4. What are three steps you can take to make that happen?

_____

_____

_____

_____

_____

5. Are there any issues in your personal life that you can work on in this season?

_____

_____

_____

_____

_____

Fun Extras!

"Untame My Heart," song by Jessie Rodgers
"Shall We Dance?," song by Amanda Wilders
"A Little Longer," song by Jenn Johnson
"Breathe," song by Jonny Diaz
"Empty," song by Wilders Worship
"Glorious Unfolding," song by Steven Curtis Chapman

God is reaching His hand out to you asking,
"Shall We Dance?"
Will you accept His invitation?

A POEM

DANCING WITH GOD

When I meditated on the word Guidance,
I kept seeing "dance" at the end of the word.
I remember reading that doing God's will is a lot like dancing.
When two people try to lead, nothing feels right.
The movement doesn't flow with the music,
And everything is quite uncomfortable and jerky.

When one person realizes that, and lets the other lead,
Both bodies begin to flow with the music.
One gives gentle cues, perhaps with a nudge to the back
Or by pressing lightly in one direction or another.
It's as if two become one body, moving beautifully.

The dance takes surrender, willingness, and attentiveness
From one person and gentle guidance and skill from the other.
My eyes drew back to the word Guidance.
When I saw "G," I thought of God, followed by "u" and "i."
"God," "u," and "i" dance. God, you, and I dance.

As I lowered my head, I became willing to trust
That I would get guidance about my life.
Once again, I became willing to let God lead.
My prayer for you today is that God's blessings
And mercies are upon you on this day and everyday.
May you abide in God, as God abides in you.

Dance together with God, trusting God to lead
And to guide you through each season of your life.
(Author unknown)

EVERY 30 SECONDS ANOTHER PERSON BECOMES A VICTIM OF HUMAN TRAFFICKING

SUPPORTING THE MINISTRY OF A21

As the author of this book, I'd like to help single women be empowered to walk in the fullness of all God has for them and to find freedom through Christ. This is not just for spiritual freedom, but physical freedom for those in bondage. A21 is a ministry I believe in that was founded by Christine Caine. I have decided to support this ministry by donating 10 percent of the proceeds from each book sold to help in their fight for freedom.

The A21 Campaign is a global anti-human trafficking organization dedicated to eradicating modern-day slavery in the twenty-first century. With eleven offices in ten countries around the world, A21 works tirelessly to rescue, restore, and rebuild the lives of human trafficking victims. Human life is invaluable, and A21 will not stop until the twenty-seven million men, women, and children trapped in slavery are set free.

A21's strategy to abolish the US$150 billion criminal industry is multi-dimensional:

Prevention: Globally, A21's goal is to stop human trafficking from ever happening in the first place by providing awareness, education to the next generation, and interrupting the demand for it.

Protection: As an organization, A21 aims to provide an environment for survivors to be safe from harm or injury. In the aftercare facilities, the girls not only receive medical care and professional counseling, but they are also given the opportunity to study a skill of their choice.

Prosecution: A21 works to prosecute traffickers, provide survivors with legal counsel and strengthen the legal response to human trafficking.

Partnership: A21 partners with local law enforcement, service providers, and community members to meet a comprehensive set of needs for those rescued from bondage. A21 couldn't fight human trafficking without the help of individuals, businesses, and organizations.

For more information or to learn how you can join the fight for freedom, go to www.a21.org.

ENDNOTES

Chapter 4 Mr. Right For You

1. Jackie Kendall, *A Man Worth Waiting For: How to Avoid a Bozo*, (New York: FaithWords, 2008.), p 25–26.

Chapter 6 En Garde!

2. Break. Dictionary.com Unabridged. Random House, Inc. <http://www.dictionary.com/browse/break>. (accessed October 2015).

Chapter 7 Standing Pure

3. Flesh Wound Dictionary.com. *The American Heritage ® Science Dictionary.* Houghton Mifflin Company. http://www.dictionary.com/browse/flesh-wound (accessed: October 2015).

4. Soul ties. <http://www.urbandictionary.com/define.php?term=soul+ties>.
   © 1999–2016 Urban Dictionary ®. (accessed November 2015).

5. Repent.Dictionary.com. *Online Etymology Dictionary.* Douglas Harper, Historian. http://www.dictionary.com/browse/repent (accessed: November 2015).

ABOUT THE AUTHOR

 Amanda Wilders grew up in O'Fallon, Missouri, and now lives in the beautiful area of Destin, Florida. She has worked over eight years in ministry and spent a year in Sydney, Australia at Hillsong International Leadership College. She is currently on staff at Destin UMC and is also one of the worship leaders for Waves Ministry, Inc., a non-profit ministry that encourages girls to make waves for Christ in their homes, community, and world. Amanda desires to share her experiences with women of all ages and help equip them to become all God has created them to be.